THE HOCKEY GOALIE'S HANDBOOK

The Authoritative Guide for Players and Coaches

Jim Corsi and John Hannon, Ph.D.

Contemporary Books

Chicago New York San Francisco Lisbon London Madrid Mexico City
Milan New Delhi San Juan Seoul Singapore Sydney Toronto

Library of Congress Cataloging-in-Publication Data

Corsi, Jim.
    The hockey goalie's handbook : the authoritative guide for players and
coaches / Jim Corsi and John Hannon.
        p.   cm.
    Includes index.
    ISBN 0-8092-9746-9
    1. Hockey—Goalkeeping.   I. Hannon, John, Ph.D.   II. Title.

GV848.76 .C67   2001
796.962′27—dc21   2001047532

Contemporary Books

A Division of The McGraw·Hill Companies

5 6 7 8 9 0   VLP/VLP   1 0 9 8 7 6 5

ISBN 0-8092-9746-9

This book was set in Sabon and Eurostile
Printed and bound by Vicks Lithograph

Cover and interior design by Nick Panos
Cover and interior photos copyright © Bill Wippert
Buffalo Sabres logo and word mark are registered trademarks of the NHL team. NHL and
team marks are the property of the NHL and its teams. Copyright © NHL. All rights
reserved.

McGraw-Hill books are available at special quantity discounts to use as premiums and
sales promotions, or for use in corporate training programs. For more information, please
write to the Director of Special Sales, Professional Publishing, McGraw-Hill, Two Penn
Plaza, New York, NY 10121-2298. Or contact your local bookstore.

This book is printed on acid-free paper.

To my father, who took me to the rink as a kid, and to Cathy, who encourages me to go to the rink as an adult

—J.C.

To my wife, who has made everything I've ever done better, and to all the dedicated men in Clinton, New York, who gave me and many other kids a passion for this game

—J.H.

Contents

Foreword

For the last three years of my 29 years as the radio play-by-play announcer for Montreal Canadiens games, Jim Corsi was the color commentator and analyst on the broadcasts. Jim brought a positive and informative approach to his job, and his grasp of the many facets of the game of hockey was obvious. But when Jim talked about goaltenders, and the art of goaltending, he turned things up a notch and was clearly in his element.

Jim's own experiences in the crease—in both North America and Europe—have given him a unique perspective on what has been called the most difficult job in team sports. His listeners, and his fellow announcer, learned much and were well entertained in the process.

I was not surprised when the Buffalo Sabres brought Jim on board to work with one of the greatest goalies in the game, Dominik Hasek. And I am not surprised that Jim has collaborated with John Hannon to produce the entertaining and insightful look at all aspects of goaltending contained in this book. It will serve as a valuable learning resource for players, coaches, and parents.

> Dick Irvin
> Member, Hockey Hall of Fame
> Pointe Claire, Quebec

Acknowledgments

We would like to thank Diane Hannon, our typist, proofreader, organizer, and helpmate; Andy Iles, Donald Byczynski, Shane Foley, Dan DeSantis, Jake Hannon, Luke Hannon, Kevin Quick, Kyle Quick, and Geoff Abrahams, who made up our cast; Rob Taylor and Craig Bolt, our top-flight editors and encouragers; Bill Wippert, our highly competent and very patient photographer; Dan Polkinghome and Louisville Hockey for supplying the goalie equipment, which was subsequently donated to the Variety Club youth hockey program for underprivileged children, in Buffalo; Marvin Mizinski and CAN-Coach for use of their excellent drill software; Brian Burke, Mary DelSignore, Deanna Hunt, and the staff at the Amherst Pepsi Center, where the photos were taken; Darcy Regier, Larry Carriere, Kevin Billet, Lindy Ruff, Don Lever, and Brian McCutcheon, members of the Buffalo Sabres' coaching and management team, who gave us the freedom to pursue this dream; Dominik Hasek, Martin Biron, Dwayne Roloson, and Mikka Noronen, great goalies; Jon Christiano, Rochester Americans, a great guy, our mutual friend, and hockey guru; Ken Ziemann, old-time goalie and passionate teacher of the game; Mike Ramsey, Minnesota Wild; Diane Charbonneau, administrative assistant; Julie Healy, Canadian Women's National Team coach; Dave Chambers, York University; Ron Ivany and Aldo Sparaciari, European Hockey experts; Rip Simonek, Jim Pizzutelli, and George Babcock, of the Buffalo Sabres' staff; Dick Irvin, hockey legend; Graeme Swan, goalie specialist; Mike Kirk, P.C.H.S.; Mickey Goulet, Ottawa University; Les Lawton, Concordia University; and Pierre Mongeon, youth hockey expert.

Introduction

"I want to be a goalie."

These may be the most frightening words a parent will ever hear. A broken window or scraped knee can be fixed relatively easily. But the emotional and financial costs that come with being a hockey goalie (and a hockey goalie's parent) add up at an alarming rate, and they can last a lifetime. "Why, oh why," you wonder.

Then it dawns on you: the exhilaration from being a hockey goalie is indescribable—and it also lasts forever. Indeed, most of the people who love this position, though we must admit it may seem a bit crazy, say that the good outweighs the bad by far.

How else can we explain the growing interest in hockey, especially the art and science of goaltending? While teams and leagues are sprouting up in the most unlikely places—beach communities in Florida, desert towns in Arizona, the Texas flatlands—the colorful and popular "United Nations" of goalies led by Belfour, Biron, Brodeur, Dafoe, Hasek, Joseph, Khabibulin, Kolzig, Luongo, Roy, Richter, and Vanbiesbrouck are quickly becoming the most recognizable players in the sport.

Not only is ice hockey growing in popularity, but in-line programs are sweeping across the land as well. In addition, there is strong growth in women's hockey where there was virtually none a mere five years ago. Universities and high schools are scrambling to add teams, while male youth organizations in Minnesota, Massachusetts, and New York are striving to replicate their programs for girls. Every one of these teams needs goalies—good goalies.

A product of our lifelong commitment to teaching, this book is designed to be *the* authoritative source for goaltending instruction for the next decade. In the pages that follow, we will teach you, your coach, and your parents to make you a better goalie. We have been trained to teach. We serve as teachers. Teaching is our mission. Quite simply, we want to teach those of you who want to be taught to be the absolute best goaltenders you can be.

The Hockey Goalie's Handbook is the most comprehensive guide that has ever been written on the subject of hockey goaltending. The ideas presented here have been accumulating and being refined for more than 30 years at the youth, college, junior, and pro levels. Our observations are based on the knowledge we have gained from scouting, studying, and coaching some of the best goalies in the world—most notably, the one and only Dominik Hasek.

Since our key themes—such as tracking, active input, body control, being in the shot lane, gap control—are repeated and built upon throughout the book, you can pick it up almost anywhere and start reading. Naturally, we would recommend reading it from cover to cover first. Then, when you need help in a particular area, you can refresh your memory by returning to the relevant chapter in the future.

From a technical and tactical standpoint, the book relies heavily on Jim Corsi's extensive firsthand knowledge of the North American and European approaches to goaltending at the professional level. Unlike many goalie coaches, even some at the NHL level, Jim has played and studied the game at the highest levels of international competition.

Over the years we have taught and coached from the bottom (mites, novices, peewees, and bantams) to the top (juniors, college, and pros) of the ladder of competitive organized hockey. Drawing on this experience, we have tried to create a book that people of all ages can learn from. That's the main purpose behind our Kid's Keys. By reading the Kid's Keys and looking at the photos, any child age six or older should be able to master the building blocks of our philosophy of goaltending. Taking this a step further, we believe that the most effective approach is for both you, the aspiring goaltender, and your coach or parent to read this book. Then the two of you will literally be on the same page—at least when it comes to goaltending, that is!

Another unique feature of this book are numerous and varied instructional lists the likes of which have never been compiled before. We recommend that you carefully study these lists, which are dispersed throughout the book. See, for example, "10 Ways to Stop Your Opponent's Momentum After a Whistle," in Chapter 8; you never know when you'll need to nudge the net off its moorings to put an end to an offensive barrage in your own end!

Great goaltending always starts with great skating. Once you can skate well, you need to be an active rather than a passive goaltender. Does that just mean to get involved in the play? No—we want you to *influence* the play. To get your team out of trouble, for example, we want you to know how—and when—to deflect a shot into the corner, or start a breakout by sending the rebound out to your teammate, or slow your opponents' momentum by freezing the puck.

This book provides you with what we call the "goalie's toolbox"—a variety of techniques for stopping the puck before it crosses that goal line behind you. Your challenge is to learn these techniques and be able to call upon them when needed. Learn them all. Master them all. There is no reason to limit yourself to being one particular type of goalie.

This is why Dominik Hasek is such a great goalie—the best in the world, in the opinion of many. Without question, Hasek has helped to redefine the position more than any other goalie. Why? Simply because he has more tools in his toolbox—and he has developed the instincts to call on the right one just when it is needed. Depending on what the game situation calls for, Hasek can make a save with his helmet and head the puck forward like a soccer player. Or catch the puck, toss it up, and bat it out of the zone like a baseball player. Or drop his stick and pick the puck up with his blocker hand. Or, while lying on his back, kick a leg here or throw an arm there.

Is Hasek just winging it out there? Absolutely not. What Hasek and others like him have done is learn new techniques and develop them. First and foremost, these techniques allow Hasek to get into position to make the save. The style and flair that accompany his saves are what casual observers usually focus on, but the fact is that he is in the proper position in the first place.

We have heard goalies, even those we are training, say things such as "I am a butterfly goalie, so why should I learn how to stack the pads?" or "Don't you understand? My goalie coach is Joe Fivehole, and he told me to do it this way." With an attitude like this, you are only limiting your potential. Don't ever fall into the trap of thinking you know all that a goalie needs to know. You must always be searching for new ways and new tools to improve your skills.

Indeed, if there are people or books out there that contradict or expand upon what we are saying, we want you to listen to what they have to say, too. That is why we have provided you, in Chapter 11, with a comprehensive list of resources. We acknowledge that some of the authorities listed there may not be properly qualified, and we don't agree with many of them on certain points. But we are educators by nature, and we want you to be an informed student of the game. Weigh their assertions and test their ideas—and add those that you find to be worthwhile to your toolbox. The better informed and educated you are in your craft, the better a goalie you will be.

1

Goaltending

Forgive us for our bias, but we believe that goaltending is truly the most important position in team sports. In goal-oriented sports, attention centers around the net. The goalie is the stopper. Sure, the top scorers are usually in the limelight, and rightly so, for without scoring, all games would end up in a tie! However, the goaltenders are what stand between those top scorers and their object—the four-by-six opening through which a puck must pass in order for a player to tally a score.

Team sports require both a team strategy and individual skills. Most often, team play is the main order of business, and the play of individuals is encompassed within that team concept. But the success of both a team and its players ultimately hinges on consistent goaltending. A forward may "just miss scoring" or a defenseman may "just miss his check"—and it is entirely possible that either of these lapses will have no bearing on the game's outcome. However, when a goalie "just misses," his lapse is immediately revealed to the world by a change in the score.

For this reason, goalies have a spotlight unlike that of any of their teammates. All players feel pressure to succeed and win, but on the ice goaltenders must respond to this pressure in a unique way. They don't have the luxury of rest during shift changes, and they can't simply skate harder to overcome weaknesses in their play. On top of that, a goalie has to deal with quick play-action changes, anticipate what his defensemen and what the opposing shooters will do, and make the proper decisions about freezing the puck and keeping it in play—all this while wearing a set of equipment that is heavier and more cumbersome than any other on the ice.

More than any other player, goalies are "full-time employees"—that is, they are called upon to use their talents and skills from the

Table 1.1 General Guide to Development: Stages by Age Group for Youth Goalies

Age	Type of Skates	Skate in Team Drills	Fielding (F) and Puck Handling (PH)	Skating Skill	Ready Stance (OZ = offensive zone)	Net Coverage: Gap-Control Angles	Play Action and Rushes	Read and React	Save Skills
4–6	All—regular.	As often as possible.	Make the first save with stick.	To learn how to move fast from point to point.	Alert stance (stick on ice, gloves up) with constant reminder.	Beginner—stay in the paint (crease).	Just play and copy your hero.	Puck is focus.	Get something in the way to make save.
7–8	House—regular. Travel—goalie.	As often as possible.	Shot on the net, push puck to side.	Increase speed. Master stops and starts forward and backward.	Alert stance (stick on ice, gloves up) with periodic reminder.	Top of crease to post.	Play and try to stay on feet. Try telescoping.	Puck and around net are focus.	Try to use the appropriate piece of equipment to make save.
9–12	All—goalie.	As often as possible, but difficult for travel teams.	F: Behind the net. PH: passing and lift puck.	Very important. Straight shuffle and T-pushes. Telescoping, some lateral.	Chosen ready stance with some reminder. Maintains somewhat during play action.	Top of crease with T-push (shuffle) to post.	Telescoping on original puck carrier. Some lateral movement moving to follow puck position.	Puck and prime off-puck player are focus.	Use right piece of equipment to make save. Develop multiple save skills.
13–16	All—goalie.	After skaters move down ice, follow doing goalie-specific skating.	F: Behind net. F: In corners. PH: Controlled pass, clearing zone, stick-handling; backhand—one-handed	Telescoping (fwd/bwd). Tracking (left/right). Lateral movement (T-shuffle).	Chosen ready stance with little reminder. Maintains during OZ play. Recovery to stance after threat.	Telescoping out of crease and return to post. Save skills during lateral movement.	Telescoping initial puck carrier. Lateral movement to track play action (some pursuit).	Current play action is focus.	Use right save skill in right situation.
17–20	All—goalie.	After skaters move down ice, follow doing goalie-specific skating.	F: Fast feet for behind-net & corner dump-ins. PH: strength; clear zone in air; hit glass; backhand high; stick handling either-handed.	Same as above with more speed and compact economy of motion.	Chosen ready stance with minimal reminder. OZ: Independent upper body and hands from legs; urgent recovery to stance.	Telescoping; constant play-action tracing; save skills lateral movement; puck pursuit.	Telescoping; lateral movement tracking. Aggressive puck pursuit. Save skill during tracking. Compact economy of motion.	Current and anticipated play action are focus.	Use right save skill in right situation. Advanced recoveries. Eliminate second chances.

opening face-off to game's end. Theirs is a demanding and difficult position that requires 100 percent focus.

Developmental Guidelines

To summarize the various stages of development for goalies, we have created the "General Guide to Development" (see Table 1.1). This profile is based on our observation of thousands of goalies over the last 30 years. We readily admit that the table is not perfect or fool-proof, and we are aware that there will certainly be exceptions to these generalities. However, the principles we outline here should apply to a great majority of goaltenders.

Position of Responsibility

Because any goal is potentially a game-winner or at least one that keeps a team in the game, the play of a goalie has more bearing on a team's success than that of any other player. A "routine" shot that is let in for a goal can destroy the goalie's self-confidence or "deflate the bench" of the scored-upon team. Indeed, sometimes players even feel betrayed by poor goaltending.

We all know that for any goal there are usually three or more mistakes preceding it, but you as the net minder must take responsibility for all goals. You cannot trot out a new excuse for every puck that gets by you: "It was tipped"; "There was a screen"; "It was a breakaway"; "The defenseman missed his check"; "I was bumped": "My own guy deflected it." These events are part of the game of hockey, and you as the goalie must be able to anticipate them.

Rather than look for excuses, try this approach instead: Look in the mirror before blaming the play of your teammates. Offer no excuses. Commit to maximizing your effort and minimizing your mistakes in the minutes, periods, games, and seasons that follow. Learn from the experience and you'll improve. It is just that simple.

Because the goalie is in such a position of great responsibility (later on, you'll see how the goalie's decision-making and communication skills are reflected in his every movement), he must have a strong belief in himself and possess excellent physical and technical abilities. His self-confidence and talent are constantly tested: remember, the game is focused on the net!

For young goalies especially, the pressure of the position can be overwhelming. Consequently, coaches have a responsibility to make sure that the game remains enjoyable for goalies even while the goalies are being instructed in the finer points of their position. For their part, goalies must be able to accept criticism if they hope to improve at their position. So coaches must carefully consider how to deliver this criticism without robbing the goalie of his self-confidence and his enjoyment of the game.

There is a saying: "The goaltender is in a team sport, playing alone." But goalies need not be loners in the team's overall defensive strategy. Yes, the goalie is "alone" while waiting for the action to develop. But the concept of team defense for most hockey teams today calls for active input on the part of goaltenders. In other words, goalies on successful teams do more than simply block pucks; they are part of the team's defensive package.

Tracking

Almost any situation can result in a shot on goal. To be successful, therefore, a goalie must continually follow the play. While tracking the play, the goalie should always be aware of the play action, constantly maintaining his position in the shot lane even if there is no shot forthcoming.

Always keep in mind that goaltending is risky business—even when your own team has the puck. Murphy's Law as applied to hockey reads like this: If it's possible to lose control of the puck, someone will! For goaltenders, therefore, there is never any time to relax.

When considering the statistic of shots on goal, remember that in a typical game there are generally 50 percent more shots directed at the net than the shots-on-goal figure indicates. In other words, if there were 24 shots on goal during a game, there were approximately 12 additional shots that missed the net. In total, 36 shots actually were directed at the net.

A high number of shots, then, doesn't necessarily mean the goalie has had a particularly difficult game. The majority of shots in regular play are generally routine saves. The most difficult saves to make are from "chances"—shots that give the shooter a great advantage when the offense has penetrated the defensive zone in critical areas—below the tops of the circles and between the face-off dots. In most contests, chances represent only a small percentage of the total shot count. But a chance can develop at any moment.

We'll discuss tracking and play action in more depth in later chapters. For now, keep in mind that the goalie must follow all movements on the ice, even when his own team has the puck. To track effectively, a goalie must be on the alert constantly!

Active Input

Save techniques are skill oriented. These skills, along with active input from the goaltender, can be an integral part of a team's overall defensive system. The "aggressive" goalie puts pressure on the shooter and on the play action of the opposing team. A goalie's development in this respect depends on his personal strength and his ability to react to challenges. Of course, the higher the level of play, the more demanding those challenges will be.

The best example of active and aggressive input can be seen in the play of Dominik Hasek. The Dominator both focuses on the puck and sees the play as it develops; that is, he "thinks like a forward but plays like a goalie." When a goalie begins to play in this way—in other words, when he shows an awareness of the team's whole defensive package—he signals the beginning of an improvement in his overall performance. Among NHL goalies, Hasek is a true innovator in this regard.

Hasek and most of the other great goalies of today, such as Patrick Roy, Ed Belfour, and Martin Brodeur, demonstrate active input in another way as well: they are students of the game. They are always trying to master new goaltending tools.

Evolution of Goaltending

One of the big themes throughout this book will be "going to the shot lane with maximum net coverage." A lesser emphasis will be placed on goaltending "style." This is because true individual style among today's top goaltenders is quickly disappearing.

What is generally understood as a goalie's "style" is the skill set the goalie uses most often. However, overuse of a skill makes a goalie predictable. To be successful, a goalie has to be able to bring other skills to bear.

At the highest levels of play (NHL and international competition), more and more goalies are blending styles. Or they have no clearly defined style. Kolzig, Brodeur, Hasek, Joseph, and Roy have different styles, and all of them are successful. Their success is attributable not so much to their style as to their skill set and their ability to select the right tool to stop the puck. Indeed, style is going out of style! Today, the biggest determinant of a goalie's success or failure is the composition of his skill toolbox.

Among these tools are covering the net area and at-puck skills. With a butterfly save, a goalie blocks and covers a large area of the net to stop the puck. With a trapper save, he moves his hand at the puck to stop it. To call forth the proper save skill, you need to develop the ability to read and react to the play action.

Because they are perplexed by it, some coaches and players have labelled this approach to goaltending unorthodox. But coaches and goalies need to understand how the goalie position is changing. *The Hockey Goalie's Handbook* acknowledges the traditional distinction between style and skill set. When we talk about style, we identify the different ready stances with the traditional terminology (stand-up, butterfly, etc.). However, we believe that these labels will become less and less useful in the future. This development will help give goalies the freedom to evolve beyond style, as Hasek has done. We believe that the future of goaltending is a blending of styles that draws on many different save skills.

So it is vitally important for young goaltenders to learn as many net area/blocking skills, at-puck/reaction skills, and skating skills as possible. Butterfly saves, stand-up techniques, paddle-down moves, puck handling, and skate-edge control are just some of the many skills today's goalies need to have in their toolbox. The multidimensional and multitalented goalie is here to stay.

10 Great Ways to Study Your Position

Instructional books

Instructional videos

Videos of your own game/practice

Watching televised games

Attending games in person

Attending good hockey schools

Watching other sports (e.g., soccer, lacrosse)

Playing other sports (e.g., soccer, lacrosse)

Teaching someone younger or less experienced than yourself

Mental self-evaluation: "seeing" yourself do better and "visualizing"
  your success

2

Off-Ice Training And On-Ice Preparation

Hockey players, like players in all sports, need to be in top physical condition. It's no different for the goaltender. Too often, however, when a team is on the ice, the goalie is left to prepare on the side. Sometimes the goalie participates in a series of "dry-land" training sessions with the team. The goaltender can use this period of pre-ice preparation to work aerobically and anaerobically and to reinforce goaltending skills.

Since we are not certified experts in physical fitness, we should add a special note here. We highly recommend that you undergo a complete physical by a doctor before beginning any fitness program. This is especially important for players at advanced levels of play.

The training you need as a hockey goaltender involves both aerobic and anaerobic activities. A word about the difference between "aerobic" and "anaerobic" exercises. The body requires specific training for certain physical activities that burn oxygen predominantly, as a fuel (aerobic); other types of training are needed for physical activities that don't burn oxygen predominantly but use other biological sources (anaerobic). The complete explanation is a lot more complicated than that, but we'll leave the specific requirements of each type of exercise to the physical fitness experts. Suffice it to say that off-ice training is fundamental to overall preparation for all athletes—including goalies.

10 Important Physical Attributes

Skating skills
Hand/eye coordination
Foot/eye coordination
Agility
Mobility
Fast feet
Physically fit (strength and conditioning)
Positive pain threshold
Quick reactions and reflexes
Balance

Stretching

Before undertaking any vigorous training program, all athletes should stretch. Stretching is the most fundamental element of goaltender preparation. To be successful, a goaltender must have good flexibility and agility, two characteristics that are enhanced by stretching exercises.

Most well-prepared coaches and athletes have their own regimen of conventional stretching routines and other techniques (proprioceptive stretching, for example). Stretching for goaltenders needn't be different from that of other players. However, since acrobatics and sudden snapping movements are standard fare for a goaltender, proper stretching is necessary to prevent injury; ultimately, it will also improve the goalie's level of skill execution.

For the most part, youth equals elasticity. Even so, young players should have a training regimen. Training early will keep young muscles flexible even when they later develop more strength and "stiffness." If possible, the stretching program should be done daily, in-season and off-season.

Off-Ice Stretching Exercises

Flexibility is key to physical preparation for all athletes—goalies included. Stretching should be controlled and done slowly and consistently, with no bouncing, jarring motions. The stretch should slightly pass your limit without pain in any other area. Hold the stretch for 5 seconds. Relax for 5 seconds between exercises. Use the stretching period to focus on the upcoming game; do some "play-action" imaging—that is, see yourself succeed during an imaginary save or play action.

Warm-Up

Warming up gets your body tissues ready for the serious activity that follows. It is important to get 5 to 10 minutes of moderate exercise—skipping rope, riding a stationary bike, or jogging lightly, for example.

Exercises

Neck stretch: Rotate your head to the left, center, right, then forward (10 times each)—do not move your head backward.

Vertical stretch: Start in a crouching position with your hands on the floor, then stretch arms above head and onto your toes. Stretch 3 times.

Hip stretch: Ten side bends, each side.

Toe touch: Stand with your legs about shoulder-width apart. Keeping your legs straight, lower your upper body toward your right knee. Hold for 5 seconds and release. Stand up and lower yourself to your left knee. Hold for 5 seconds and release. Repeat each side 2 more times.

Lower-back and hamstring stretch: Sit with your legs spread apart. Reach with your right hand to your left knee. Bring your chest down to your knee for 5 seconds. Return to a sitting position and hold for 5 seconds. Reach over with your left hand and grab your right foot.

Vertical stretch

Hip stretch

Lower your chest down to your knee for 5 seconds. Repeat 3 times. Don't be too rigid with your knees.

Side lunges: Stand straight with your feet shoulder-width apart and your toes pointing ahead. With your hands on your waist, lunge left, stand up, and then lunge right. Hold each position for 5 seconds and repeat 3 times.

Quadriceps stretch: Standing on your left leg, reach back with your right hand, grab your right foot, and pull it toward your buttocks. (Use a wall for balance, if necessary.) Hold 5 seconds and release. Do the same with your left leg. Repeat 3 times on each side.

Hip adductor and abductor stretch: In a sitting position with the soles of your feet pressed together, push your knees apart with your hands resisting and hold 5 seconds. Then do the opposite movement: pull your knees together with your hands resisting. Repeat each stretch 3 times.

Toe touch and hamstring stretch

Lower-back and hamstring stretch

Groin stretch and side lunge

Quad stretch

Back stretch: On your hands and knees, bring your left knee toward your chin and then stretch your leg out full length; hold each for 5 seconds. Repeat 3 times for each leg.

Split stretch: From a standing position, bend down and slowly stretch to extended leg position. Repeat 3 times for each side.

Hip flexor and hamstring stretch: Kneel on one knee and support with your hands, then lightly lean back. Hold 5 seconds and then extend your leg slowly and bring your head to your knee. Repeat 3 times for each side.

Pregame Stretching Exercises

This is the most important exercise for all players. Stretching prepares muscles for work and reduces possible injury. As with all athletes, the more flexible and agile a goalie is, the better his range of skills will be. Choose any five of the previous stretches and make them part of your pregame preparation. To get the best results, focus on your lower back and legs.

Abductor and adductor stretch (groin)

Back stretch

Splits and hamstring stretch

Hip flexor and hamstring stretch

We suggest that you try a set that includes the following stretches: toe touch, side lunges, quadriceps stretch, hip adductor and abductor, hip flexor, and hamstring stretch. When you are stretching, try to visualize yourself in game situations and call up images of yourself succeeding (making the big save, being congratulated by your teammates after a win, etc.).

Strength and Weight Training

As mentioned previously, peak physical fitness is necessary for athletic activity. A proper blend of aerobic, anaerobic, and strength-training preparation can be achieved with professional guidance. Stretching is important and necessary for proper performance. Done properly, weight training can be valuable, but there are differing opinions about weight training for goalies. To be sure, goaltending requires strength, especially when one considers that the goalie equipment itself weighs from 30 to 40 pounds. But weight training also builds muscle mass, so a goalie has to see to it that his new "strength" does not interfere with his flexibility and agility. In general, a goalie can achieve the strength he needs with light weights and repetitive training; there is no need to bulk up. Muscle mass can slow a goalie and impede his play: strong muscles that are quick and reactive enhance a goalie's play.

If weight training is to be part of a goalie's off-ice training, professionals can help the coach and the goalie understand weight-training specifics for the goaltender position and develop a suitable program. Remember that weight training is age-sensitive—as a rule of thumb, for prepubescent players such training should rely on resistance training utilizing body weight as a countervailing force (sit-ups, push-ups, chin-ups, piggyback rides, wheelbarrow rides, etc.). Having seen many a farm boy throw bales of hay from a young age without any adverse effects, we are a little less cautious in this area than some others are.

Jogging, running, stops and starts, skipping rope, mountain biking, stationary biking, and weight training can all be of enormous benefit in dry-land training sessions. It's important to drink plenty of water during training (as well as during games—keep a water bottle on top of the net). A proper balance of goalie-specific exercises can address conditioning, coordination, and save techniques. Without question, off-ice training will enhance a goalie's overall game preparedness.

Off-Season Program

The preseason, or "summer," program is the goalie's opportunity to prepare for training camp. Weights are sometimes used to increase strength for specific muscle groups. This is a personal choice, and as mentioned previously, it calls for professional advice. A goaltender should concentrate on flexibility, strength, and cardiorespiratory endurance. We suggest a summer program done over an 8-to-12-week period—a program that gradually increases resistance and repetitions and, because there are no weights involved, carries minimal risk of injury. You may want to ask your coach and family about workouts that include weight training with the proper oversight.

The workout program uses the athlete's body weight and increasing repetitions to effect an increase in resistance. If the repetitions, or "reps," are too much initially, you can reduce the number that you do. The same goes for "timed" exercises (especially cardio and aerobic workouts)—work out for fewer seconds each interval. Basically, start "lowly and slowly."

Remember our cautionary note at the start of this chapter: Before embarking on any exercise regimen, check with your family doctor or your team doctor to establish your level of fitness. And if you experience any pain during a workout, especially chest pain, stop your routine and see the doctor immediately!

In-Season Program

During the season, games are your first priority. It is always difficult to balance time among games, practices, travel, family, school, and other commitments. To compound this problem, finding available ice for practice is sometimes difficult. However, if you can manage to continue with portions of the preseason workout program, that is an excellent way to maintain your level of fitness—and will, in turn, maximize your abilities on the ice.

We suggest that you choose one or two exercises from each of the following programs and do them religiously. Ideally, you should perform these development exercises, as opposed to mere maintenance exercises, two to three times a week. Make sure to take adequate time to recover, especially during those intense periods when your schedule is filled with games, practice, and travel.

Stretching: Stretch before beginning any serious workout, and warm up properly. Stretching should be done daily during both the hockey season and the off-season.

Free Body/Body Resistance: Exercises such as sit-ups, chin-ups, and push-ups are good "free-body" workouts. Do not overtrain; injuries can result from too many repetitions. Start with 5 reps and work your way up. Repeat 2 to 3 times weekly during the season and daily in the off-season.

Blocks Workout: Interval training with blocks has many variations. The six push-up exercises in Table 2.1 are goalie-oriented, each one concentrating on a specific muscle group. Start with 3 reps per station. Repeat the cycle of six exercises 3 times with a 15-second rest between each station. When your strength increases, increase the number of reps equally per station. Control your breathing—exhale "up" and inhale "down." These exercises should be done every other day during the preseason. In-season you'll need to check your game schedule, but twice weekly is usually a good maintenance scheme.

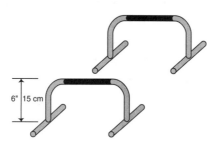

"Blocks"

Aerobics: To develop cardiorespiratory endurance, there are many options. Jogging, stationary biking, hiking, mountain biking, skipping rope, plyometrics, and running stairs are all good cardio workouts. The important thing to remember is that, to be effective, an aerobic workout should last at least 20 to 25 minutes daily or every other day. (Check with your doctor for the proper heart rate for your gender, age, and fitness level.) We recommend skipping rope, especially for preseason programs; it's an excellent aerobic workout that requires endurance, speed, and coordination.

Table 2.1 Six Blocks Exercises

Muscle Area	Position of Blocks	Method/Comments
Shoulders	Shoulder width I I	elevate feet for maximum shoulder work
Shoulders (angled)	╱ ╲	increases shoulder flexibility
Chest	⊢ ⊣	works the chest
Triceps (inner)	I I	works the arms
Triceps (outer)	I I	sit between blocks with legs extended
Back	⊢ ⊣	works both back and "glutes"

Weight training: As a guideline, three times a week is a good regimen (for example, you can train Monday, Wednesday, and Friday and take an extra day off at the end of the week); but keep in mind that the type and frequency of lifting is a function of age. Don't omit your warm-up, stretching, sit-ups (abdominals), push-ups, and cool-down. Note that weight-training exercises can be used also for advanced-level training. However, advanced-level training may be too demanding for youths and "weekend warriors." Keep in mind that getting fit takes time and is a gradual process. Always consult an expert before beginning a weight-training program. Also, remember to drink plenty of fluids (water or sports drink) before, during, and after your workouts.

Comprehensive Dry-Land Program

Dry-land (off-ice) training helps build the proper on-ice mechanics and improve a goalie's endurance, strength, flexiblilty, and coordination. We suggest doing these exercises three times weekly in the preseason and one to two times per week during the season. (*Helpful hint:* The buddy system often works well here. Find a goalie friend who is committed and wants to work out with you. And remember to drink water or a sports drink before, during, and after the workouts.)

Warm-up: Jog lightly, skip rope, or ride a bike for 5 to 10 minutes. Do all of the stretching exercises—from head to toe—covered at the beginning of this chapter.

Goalie-specific exercises: From the following list, do the odd numbers one day and the even numbers the next.

1. Run backward and forward (in goalie position) between two chairs that are three or four meters apart (3 reps or 20 seconds).
2. Wheelbarrow for 30 yards (25 meters) and then switch with a partner (3 reps).
3. In goalie position, kick one leg out (alternating left and right; front and sideways; 5 reps each).
4. Squeeze a tennis ball in your stick hand (one minute).
5. Bounce a tennis ball off a wall from stick hand to glove hand; change hands (10 reps for each hand).
6. With two players facing a wall (one behind the other), bounce a ball off the wall while alternating positions (back throws, front catches, alternate on the catch).
7. Forward somersault; bounce ball off the wall; catch ball (3 reps).
8. Stops and starts with gloves and stick in goalie position (5 to 10 meters) (3 reps or 20 seconds).
9. Stick-handle tennis ball, alternating from forehand to backhand, with stick hand only (45 to 60 seconds).
10. Line up five tennis balls: backhand each ball with goal stick (stick hand only). Repeat: forehand each ball with goal stick (stick hand only).
11. Goalie drops to knees and then pops up. Throw tennis ball against a wall and catch (30 seconds).
12. Hold a weight in your glove hand and move the hand in simulated catching movements. Repeat in blocker hand (20 seconds).
13. At a safe distance (30 feet or more), "pepper" the goalie with 15 waist-high shots with tennis balls, using a tennis racket or hockey stick. The goalie should be equipped with a jock ("cup"), face mask, gloves, and stick. Adjust speed of shots to the goalie's age and ability.
14. Place two chairs side by side 6 feet (2 meters) apart. Goalie runs out 10 yards (9 meters) from one chair and then backs into the

other chair, always in goalie position with gloves and stick (30 seconds).

Strength and Conditioning: Concentrate on abdominals (sit-ups), chin-ups (arms and back), and push-ups (see "Blocks Workout" and "Free Body/Body Resistance" in the preceding section). The athlete's finess level should determine the number of repetitions (increase the number as strength improves). Again, keep in mind our rule: start lowly and slowly. Skip rope, ride a stationary bike, or jog for 20 minutes or more (see "Aerobics" in preceding section).

Cool Down: After any exercise, always stretch out those muscles so they don't tighten up. Replenish your lost fluids by drinking water or a sports drink.

Your Program

Ice time is too costly a commodity to be used for conditioning exercises that can be done on dry land. The exercises described above will help you take advantage of your training time off the ice to build your overall fitness. Combined with good on-ice preparation, conscientious off-ice training will result in markedly enhanced performance over the long haul.

19

To summarize, off-ice goaltender preparation should include strength, flexibility, and agility training. This will enhance the goaltender's on-ice performance and reduce the possibility of injury. Make a plan. Set realistic goals. Map out your calendar. Select the exercises best suited to you. Find a friend to work out with if you can. Work hard and keep track of your results.

On-Ice Preparation

A goalie should stretch on the ice as well as off. Unfortunately, after your off-ice stretch, 20 minutes may have gone by while you were getting dressed for the practice or game. If possible, find an open area after getting dressed and do your on-ice stretches just before hitting the ice. Once you are on the ice, a good two-to-five-minute skate (intervals of forward and backward skating) will get your circulation going. Many youth leagues don't allow much ice time for warm-ups, so be prepared and use your available time properly; for example, do a quick skate around your own zone, a couple of leg stretches, and some warm-up shots, and then stretch again just before the game starts.

Warm-Up Stretches

Here are five on-ice warm-up stretches:

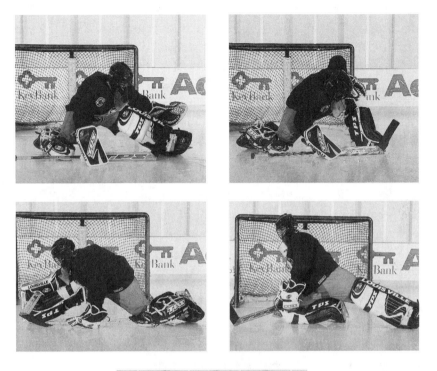

Pregame Preparation

Most players have their own on-ice pregame rituals. Whatever your ritual, it is important that you perform a complete warm-up. The old saying is still true: five minutes of warm-up is better than five days of recovery. Time permitting, pick a quiet spot on the ice (by the bench is usually good) and stretch. Essential warm-up areas are the groin (inner thigh), the thighs (quadriceps), the hips, the back, the torso, and the eyes. Generally speaking, skaters do a longer warm-up skate than goalies. After your warm-up skate, and while the rest of the players are doing theirs, you should do your stretches.

While stretching, don't forget to get your eyes and brain going, too. To prepare your eyes, focus on the players' movement as they skate around. Your eye muscles will warm up as they follow the players skating closer and farther, slower and faster. Do this while you are performing your on-ice stretch. Now you are ready to face shots or begin practice—that is, get fully involved with the on-ice activities.

When it comes to shots, the ideal warm-up is to take controlled shots from stationary/set positions so that you can get a feel for the puck. Ideally there would be some sequence, such as trapper, blocker, left leg, right leg, stick. Next, you would switch to shots off the fly with players moving.

But seldom is there enough time for a sequence like this, and most coaches want to have their players skating during the warm-up anyway. Most coaches work on team and individual needs to maximize the warm-up. But a coach needs to make it clear to his team during the warm-up that the goalie has to be exposed to quality shots to acquire a feel for the puck. Neglecting the goalie during the warm-up makes it more likely that he will surrender an early goal.

Make sure to check your equipment after the warm-up and before the game starts. If you detect a problem, speak up immediately—tell your teammates, coach, and the referee. Also, check the net. Are the pegs that hold it in place on the ice fastened? Is the net secure? You will perform better if the net cannot freely slide about. For example, without the pegs you can't use the net as an anchor (to hold on to or push off of). Also, check for any obvious holes in the net, and make sure there are no pucks in the net from the warm-ups.

To summarize, a good warm-up routine includes the following steps:

1. Stretch and play catch without equipment for 10 or 15 minutes off-ice.

2. Stretch in your equipment outside the locker room for the 5 minutes leading up to taking the ice.
3. Skate for 2 or 3 minutes (time permitting) upon taking the ice. Use this time to rough up the crease if you like.
4. Use the remaining time to take productive warm-up shots (hit the net, no dekes, no head shots).

When You Are the Backup

If you are the backup goalie for the game about to be played, you still have a very important role to play. You can help your teammates get ready to play by psyching them up. Also, you and your goal-tending partner may want to develop a routine for pumping each other up.

On the bench during the game, you should be vocal and involved in the game. Make mental or, even better, written notes of how the goals were scored—for both teams. Most coaches will welcome your comments on the other goalie's play. As you concentrate and develop a keen eye for the game, you'll even begin to see things that your coach or teammates may not.

Some coaches will actually assign the backup goalie the task of charting shots, scoring chances, and/or goals. This is an excellent way to learn and contribute. Furthermore, if you are called upon to play, you'll already be in the flow of the game.

Even if you are not scheduled to play, take the pregame warm-up seriously—you never know when you'll be asked to enter the game, and when you are, you probably won't be allowed a warm-up. At the end of each period, if possible, do some hard skating while the Zamboni is coming onto the ice. As soon as you know you'll be entering the game, start stretching on the bench or on the ice (if the other goalie has been injured, an injury time-out will have been called). Take as much time as the referee allows you.

Once the puck is dropped, be as active as you can while the puck is not in your zone. Do some skating and "up-and-downs." After each of the first several whistles, you may even want to do some sprints or more rigorous activities. Although you seldom see it on TV because the cameras are pointed elsewhere, most NHL goalies skate, simulate saves, or visualize during stoppages in play.

3

Equipment

Most goalies know about their gear—how to buy it, wear it, and use it—but not all do. A coach or parent may also not be completely sure about the goalie's equipment. So let's spend some time discussing those pillows on the goalie's legs, the suit of armor covering his chest, and the various other sources of protection available to a goalie.

The Basic Equipment

A goalie's equipment is entirely different from that of other players, which makes the role of goaltender that much more distinct. The goalie's gear is actually a series of small and large sections of "armor"—and, indeed, it looks as cumbersome and heavy as a knight's armor. Yet synthetics and other new materials have reduced the weight of the equipment and improved its flexibility and maneuverability.

In today's game of hockey, goalies are active members of the play, whether they are stopping pucks or fielding loose pucks. Fast play action and quick, hard shots are the order of the day at all levels of hockey. As a goalie, therefore, you want lightweight equipment that gives you as much range of motion as possible. To be successful, a goalie needs quick reactions when he is turning away shots and "fast feet" when he is trying to recover. Although strong legs and proper conditioning are still the number-one prerequisite for effective goaltending, the lighter equipment available today has helped goalies enormously.

Of course, a case of diminishing returns applies to goalies. Lighter gear may increase speed and movement, but it may also mean more risk of injury from high-speed pucks or heavy "traffic" in front of the net. When selecting equipment, always consider the level of play, and never trade off protection for price. Shop around for equipment;

often good bargains can be found. Remember, too, that proper care can prolong the usable lifetime of your equipment. And keep in mind that if equipment is selected properly, the player who uses it may stay interested in the game longer.

10 Biggest Equipment Problems

Forgotten piece of equipment
Skates—too big or too small; not sharpened
Lenses/eyeglasses—don't have or not used
Pads—too big
Chest protector—too big or too stiff
Trapper—too big or not broken in; too stiff
Blocker—too big
Stick—too long, too big a curve, wrong-way curve
Mask—too sophisticated, ill-fitting, too heavy
Jersey—too small

Often children are attracted by the goalie's equipment itself, so off they go into the nets. Even adults may have a desire to get between the pipes just to see what it's like. But ultimately it's *how long* one wants to keep playing the position that matters. Whatever a person's reasons for playing—or long-term commitment to the position—goaltending requires adequate protection. Getting stung by a puck because of poor protection can change a person's mind about playing in the nets. Conversely, not worrying about getting stung during action surely results in better play, because it allows the goalie to concentrate on the job at hand.

Obviously, equipment is just one of many elements in goaltending. But knowing the proper uses of each piece of equipment will improve your decision making as a goalie, whether it's knowing what gear to buy or knowing what piece of gear to use when making a save.

As we've noted, today's hockey equipment features new materials and construction that affords good protection and maneuverability. But you have to be careful when selecting equipment to buy—and this is as true of goaltender gear as any other. Equipment that is too big or cumbersome will only slow the goalie down. Equipment that is too light (or not adequate for the level of play) may make the goalie quicker, but it may also expose him to injury. You should look for equipment that will fit the player for at least a year or two. (We're aware that when it comes to equipment, goaltending is the most

If you are a left-handed-catching goalie, you'll hold your stick with your right hand and catch with your left.

expensive position in hockey. However, it bears repeating: never trade off proper protection to save money!)

Before we look at the individual pieces of a goalie's gear, we should state clearly the difference between left- and right-handed goaltenders. A *left-handed*-catching goalie has the blocker on the right hand and the trapper on the left hand. A *right-handed*-catching goalie has the blocker on the left hand and trapper on the right hand. It's easy to get confused about this when selecting and purchasing equipment, so make sure your salesperson knows what you need. Express your needs clearly with a statement such as "The trapper is on the left hand."

Underwear

Like other players on the team, the goalie should have proper undergarments, ones that are best suited for the "weather" of the rink. Turtlenecks and thermal underwear help in very cold rinks. Alternatively, light underwear is suitable for air-conditioned arenas. Whatever type you wear, remember that if you are boiling or freezing, your performance will be affected.

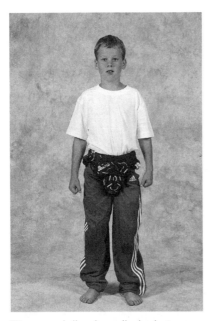

The specialized goalie jockstrap and cup give you better and more protection than a conventional one.

Goalie pants are baggier and wider than skating players' pants. The insertable pads tend to be thicker, too.

A word about caring for undergarments: washing and properly drying the underwear is not only good hygiene, it prolongs the useful lifetime of the garment.

Jock or Jill

The jockstrap and cup—the female player's version is called a "Jill"—protects a vital area of the body. Of course, the cup size depends on the age of the player. Generally speaking, the goalie's cup is more padded than a normal one, and offers protection over a wider area—from high in the inner thighs to the extreme lower part of the belly. Make sure it fits well; it should not flap around and it should allow you to maneuver on the ice without discomfort. Don't *ever* play without this piece of equipment. In fact, some goalies at higher levels wear two cups, a regular one under their goalie-specific one.

Knee Pads

When you bend your legs, your hockey pants will lift up and your leg pads will descend, exposing the area around the knee. This is the area that knee pads are designed to protect. Knee pads are optional pieces of equipment that protect the kneecap and the area of the leg four to six inches above it. Most new leg pads have (sometimes as an option) special knee padding already sewn inside. Proper-fitting pants can also reduce exposure of the knee area. Some goalie pants incorporate a knee pad extender.

Team Socks, Garters, Sweatpants

Depending on the goalie, different combinations of these garments are used—and for many different reasons (ranging from comfort to superstitions). Unless there is a team dress code that prohibits it, these pieces of equipment are selected by the goalie based on personal preference. Your legs will get very hot during play, so don't overdress by doubling, or tripling, the layers of clothing you wear.

Pants

Pants should fit properly and afford both mobility and protection. They should protect the outer thigh, the inner thigh (they should close the gap between the thighs), the hip (for sliding and sidelong spills), the tailbone, and the kidney area. Pants can last a long time, especially if they are cared for properly.

The thigh pads on goalie pants are generally twice as thick, more square, and flatter (for a truer and larger stopping surface) than those found in regular hockey pants. Special goalie pants should be considered when a goalie reaches 10 to 12 years of age. Until then, youth-hockey goalies can find sufficient protection using regular hockey pants. Above all, make sure they fit: the pant bottom should fully cover the knee when the player is in a kneeling position.

Some pants come with attached knee pads. (These are especially popular with butterfly goalies at higher levels of competition.) Some lace directly to the knee, whereas others just hang in front of the knee. Most pants are held up by suspenders, although some goalies prefer newer models that require a belt. Your preference in this regard will dictate how your chest and arm pads are worn—either tucked inside or left outside the pants.

Skates

You've probably seen youngsters play goal while wearing regular skates. This is not necessarily a problem, especially at levels of competition where pucks are not shot at a high speed.

Goalie skates are much different from other players' skates. Among other things, they feature extra plastic protection where pucks are likely to hit.

But at levels where a shot can result in injury, goalie skates should be worn. A parent should consider goalie skates for a youngster between the ages of 7 and 8 (Squirt/Novice level). At this age and up, many children are strong enough to injure another player with a shot.

Goalie skates are very different from the skates worn by other players. The boot is generally only ankle high, which affords more flexibility and the "fast feet" that are essential for hockey goalies. The boot of the goalie skate is covered by a hard plastic shell that caps the toe and extends the length of the instep (up to the laces). On the other side, this shell extends high around the anklebone and covers the heel and back of the foot.

The blade of the goalie skate is also different from those found on regular skates. It is longer, lower, and flatter, which means it has more surface contact with the ice. It is also much thicker and stronger than an ordinary skate blade. A puck traveling at high speed would bend an ordinary blade, but most goalie skate blades can withstand the impact of a shot puck.

As we will see when we discuss skating and save skills, a goalie needs sharp skate edges for many maneuvers. Skates should be sharpened regularly—at least every two to three weeks (we generally recommend once a week)—by a qualified, experienced person (there may be such a person in your area). How often you sharpen your skates will depend on how much you use them, the condition of the ice on which you play, and your level of competition. Of course, if you are in the habit of walking across the locker-room floor in your skates, you will probably have to sharpen the blades often.

How sharp should your blade be? Generally speaking, that depends on how you play. Many of today's goaltenders are active participants in the game—they do more than just stop pucks—and hence they must have fast feet, which allow a goalie to start and stop quickly, execute precise reactions, and regain his balance before a shooter gains an advantage. Remember, even a split second of extra reaction time by a goalie can give a shooter a big advantage.

A blade's "edges" are its sharp inside and outside surfaces. We prefer blade sharpening that creates an upside-down "V" (sometimes referred to as a "hollow" or "concave")—with the inside edge being the one on the instep of the skate. Others prefer angled edges that provide even more "bite" into the ice. As with so much else involving hockey equipment, personal preference is the rule here.

Experiment and see what feels best for you. Keep in mind that if a blade is too sharp, it tends to stick to the ice. And don't forget that hard ice—like outdoor ice in extreme northern climates—takes the edge off a skate quicker than any other ice surface and requires well-sharpened skates.

A special note about goalie skates: The first time you wear them, they may feel awkward and you may think you have to learn how to skate all over again. Don't despair: over time, as you work at your skating exercises, you will get accustomed to the skates.

31

Leg Pads

These are the big "pillows" that a goalie wears on his legs from toe to thigh. (I'm sure many of you recall using bedroom or couch pillows for pads when you were youngsters—much to your mother's dismay.) The leg pads are very important pieces of the goalie's gear, because a great many shots are directed at the bottom half of the net.

Today, most leg pads are made of synthetic materials. New materials and construction methods allow for easy shaping, or "working in," of the pads in accordance with the body and movements of the goalie. Custom-made leg pads are also available; of course, these pads are more costly than the conventional type.

Leg pads come in a variety of shapes (there are usually size restrictions, however—check with your league). Always remember that the "long roll," on the side of the pad, goes on the *outside* of the leg.

Because of new materials and better construction, today's leg pads are more maneuverable and provide better protection. Generally, the

Goalie pads provide you with front protection from toe to thigh, as well as side and back protection for your calves.

pad should protect from the toe of the skate (often tied in and around the toe cap) to a spot four to ten inches above the knee. Some pads have kneecap protectors attached on the inside. Others have flaps for inner-thigh and ankle-to-calf protection. These flaps on the inside of the pad are usually optional. If possible, purchase pads that have these extras.

Leg pads see a lot of work and tend to get extremely wet. Moreover, pucks, sticks, and knee drops all tend to wear down the pads. How can the pads' life be prolonged? If possible, let the pads dry between uses. Also, immediately fix any tears in the pads so the tears don't worsen. Your shoe-repair shop may be able to do this for you.

Chest and Arm Pads

Protection of the torso is very much a matter of personal choice, especially at the higher levels of competition. The "one-piece" (chest and arm pads are one) is the most popular at all levels. Many leagues at the minor hockey level supply equipment to young goalies, so don't be too surprised if you are given "mix-and-match" equipment (chest, belly, and arm pads as separate pieces of gear). Whatever the type, it is important that padding for the chest and arm areas have the following characteristics: good fit; good mobility, so as not to inhibit flexibility; and, of course, good protection to minimize injuries.

Combination chest and arm protectors are designed to allow you freedom of movement while offering maximum protection at the same time.

Chest pads should fit high enough to protect your collarbones and shoulders; be wide enough to cover the chest, belly, and side rib area; and be long enough to cover your hip points over the pants. Some players like to tuck the chest pad inside the pants and place the pants' suspenders over the chest pad, but be aware that the chest pad will push up when you move if it is tucked inside the pants. Other players like to use a belt to keep the pants snug. Whether or not you should tuck the chest pad into the pants is strictly a matter of your personal comfort. It also depends on how mobile and secure you feel. You'll know what to do only by trying different methods.

Arm padding should protect the forearm, the elbow (the outer point of the elbow as well as the inside of the joint), and the upper arm and shoulder caps extending to the collarbones just under the throat.

The blocker (left) is used primarily to deflect pucks, while the trapper (right) is used to catch and smother pucks.

The Blocker

The blocker glove, which is worn on the stick hand, is a large rectangular shape with the back of the glove facing the shooter. Most gloves these days have finger protections and thumb covers for shots that "crawl" up the stick. The rectangular area on most late-model blockers has curved sections to help control deflections.

The blocker is used mainly for deflecting pucks; used in conjunction with the trapper, it is effective for smothering pucks as well. Because of the goalie's natural stance, the blocker "hand" really consists of two pieces of equipment: the blocker and the stick. When selecting a blocker, make sure that it affords maneuverability. It must be snug around the wrist, yet allow you to angle pucks to the corner without twisting your wrist excessively. Keep in mind that a goalie's stick-handling and puck-control abilities are directly related to how manageable his blocker is.

The Trapper

This glove, which is used to catch pucks, is often referred to as a "catcher." Like the blocker, this glove sees a lot of action and has many uses. Some young goalies tend to forget this and are content merely to get the glove on the shot. This can result in a rebound that an opponent easily puts into the goal.

When selecting a trapper, remember that bigger is not necessarily better. We have all seen youngsters struggle to play baseball with oversized mitts. This problem is not as easy to spot with goalies because of all the other equipment, but it can be just as severe. There is no reason for getting a trapper the size of a bushel basket! If the trapper is too big, a youngster won't be able to stick-handle with it, let alone move it into position or catch pucks with it once it is in position. On the other hand, a trapper that is too small or light may not protect the goalie's hand from injury.

These days, many trappers have "cheaters" (extensions of the cuff to the thumb) and extra-deep pockets, or webs. Every little bit of extra protection helps—but remember: a trapper that is so big that it does not allow your hand to get to the puck quickly is of no use to you at all. Your main concern should be making sure the glove fits and is suitable to level of play. Also, be aware that most professional leagues and some leagues at lower levels place restrictions on trapper size. Check with your coaches to make sure your trapper conforms to league rules.

Trapper manufacturers are improving construction methods, and these days gloves are more flexible and easier to close. However, most new gloves are stiff and have to be "worked in" before they feel right to a goalie and can be quickly opened and closed. You can accelerate this process by placing a puck or two in the pocket of the glove and tightly wrapping a lace around the entire glove. Do this immediately after a practice, and don't unwrap the lace until you are ready to use the glove again.

Before, during, and after games, always make sure that the trapper's basket and laces are intact. This should be part of a routine check of all your equipment. You don't ever want to be betrayed by faulty gear.

The Stick

The goalie stick has three main purposes: to stop pucks along the ice, to make passes, and to clear pucks. Active goaltending requires good puck-handling skills. Like a tennis player, Dominik Hasek often bats the puck the length of the ice. Recently, several NHL goalies have even fired the puck the length of the ice and scored goals.

Goalie sticks have different lies. When the blade of the stick is kept flat on the ice, depending on the lie, your stick will force you to stand more upright or more crouched.

So good stick selection is critical. This has led to goalies pushing stick designs to the limits to serve specific needs. Curves, rockers, bent shafts, different "lies," rubber grips, and various taping techniques have almost reinvented the goalie stick. Yet some goalies select their sticks for the wrong reasons—like the desire to have a better shot.

But, as we'll see, there are drawbacks to many features of stick design. The more curved the blade of your stick is, the more difficult it is to put the entire blade of the stick on the ice. When you have a stick with a big curve and the heel is put down, the toe of the stick rises off the ice. Similarly, when the toe is put flush to the ice, the heel comes up. This is why we recommend a virtually straight stick, especially for young goalies who may not need to take advantage of a stick's curve to fire the puck high out of the zone.

The strength and speed of most older goalies compensate for any ice coverage that is lost owing to the curvature of the blade. Some goalies catch left-handed but stick-handle like a right-handed skater (Jim does this). A left-handed curve presents difficulties in this scenario. NHLer Dwayne Roloson is the best cross-handed puck handler. He can shoot or pass either left-handed or right-handed—and he does so with authority.

Some sticks these days incorporate two curves into the shaft. One of these curves, the one where the shaft meets the paddle, is where you hold your stick. Holding the stick here leaves your fingers and wrist in a more natural and comfortable position. The second curve is at the top of the shaft. The purpose of this curve is to allow more space for your fingers to slide under the stick if it is lying flat on the ice or to make the knob more easily accessible if the stick is flipped over on the other side. Many of today's sticks also have a lightweight rubber grip where the paddle and shaft meet; this grip allows for better grasp and control of the stick.

A goalie's stick affects his stance, so sticks should be selected with an eye toward the stick's weight, the shaft's overall length, the length of the paddle and the built-up section of the shaft, and the stick's lie. Younger goalies should pay particular attention to the stick's overall weight and feel.

The top of the shaft should be at about shoulder height, or two to three inches above, when you are in the ready stance with your skates on (or about six inches above shoulder height with your skates off). A strip of electrical tape can be placed along the bottom of the stick blade to protect it against premature wear. The entire blade should be covered with friction tape for better puck control.

A large circular knob of tape should be placed at the top of the stick (plastic, reusable knobs are available). This allows you to easily recover the stick if it is dropped. It also allows you to more easily keep your hold on the stick when it is thrust forward for a poke check. The knob and paddle on today's sticks are changing to reflect the paddle-down skills so much in evidence these days. The knob is essentially a half-knob, which allows a goalie to more easily get the whole stick flush to the ice, whereas the paddle is shaved or contoured so the goalie's fingers don't touch the ice.

A stick's "lie" is the angle between the blade and the shaft. The closer the angle is to 90 degrees when the blade is flat on the ice, the higher the lie; conversely, the closer the angle is to 180 degrees, the lower the lie. The lie of your stick should put your stick-side elbow at a comfortable height when you are in your normal goalie stance. Youth goalies should look for a stick with a lie between 12 and 14.

If possible, select one brand and model of stick and stay with it for at least a season. (This goes for your other equipment, too. With the exception of sticks, which can be changed annually, it is wise to stay with an equipment manufacturer and model series for several years in a row. When it comes to equipment, consistency and familiarity are important.)

Face Mask

"Face mask" means both face and full head protection. Thankfully, the face mask has continued to be used by goalies since the late, great Jacques Plante first popularized it.

There are basically three types of face masks: face-molded (not seen too often today), cage and helmet, and part molded and part cage.

The face-molded mask is fitted to the face of the wearer. The best type of molded mask is made to measure—that is, it fits the wearer's face precisely. The mask should have a back plate to protect the back of the head. Although the face-molded mask is expensive, it generally provides a good level of protection. It is no longer widely used anymore because it is usually heavier and retains heat longer.

The helmet and cage is Dominik Hasek's face mask of choice; we prefer it as well. The helmet on this type of mask is like a forward's helmet, but attached to it is a heavy wire cage that covers the face, chin, and ears. This type of mask provides great head and face protection, affords good visibility, and allows for good cooling. It is the best choice of head protection for goalies, especially young ones.

A recent—and very good—improvement in masks is the form-fitted, molded helmet with cage. The mask can be fashioned from either a face mold or a prefabricated mold. A large opening from the eyebrow area to just under the nose is covered by a wire cage. Like

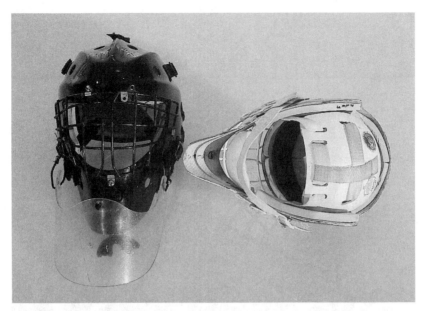

Goalie masks are composed of a padded plastic helmet, a wire mask, a padded plastic back plate, and a hinged, hanging throat guard.

the face-molded mask, it should have a back plate to which a neck guard is affixed. Overall, this mask affords good visibility and protection.

This type of mask is very popular right now—a main reason being that Dominik Hasek uses it. Another reason for its popularity is that it can be customized with drawings, decals, and the like. One problem with this feature is that youth goalies may need to change masks every year if they switch teams.

Today, the vast majority of face masks are either helmet/cage or molded/cage masks. We recommend the helmet/cage variety for players at the youth level. But be aware that some leagues place restrictions on the size of the openings in cage masks. Check with your league before buying.

Throat Protection

It is difficult to overestimate the importance of throat protection. Getting hit in the throat by a puck traveling at high speed can result in very serious injury.

There are different types of equipment used for protecting goalies' throats: Bib-style protectors hang from the chin area of the mask. U-

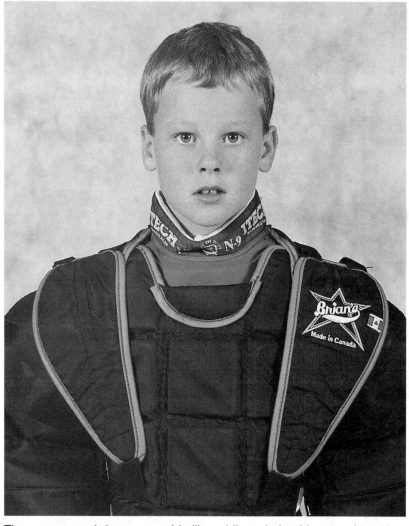

The wraparound throat guard is like a bib and should cover the only remaining vulnerable areas on your body—your upper chest and neck.

style protectors hang from the sides of the mask like a big smile. Wraparound throat guards, most of which are made of ballistic nylon covering a layer of rigid plastic plates, cover the area from the top of the throat down to the collarbone.

We recommend that goalies use the mask-affixed and the neck-adhered types simultaneously. Each type provides protection from pucks and sticks. The neck-adhered wrap provides protection from skates as well. All Canadian leagues mandate the use of both types, so you don't have much room for personal choice. It should be so everywhere.

Getting Dressed

Younger goalies (ages 5 through 10) shouldn't feel embarrassed getting help tying their skates and strapping on their pads. After all, some of the world's highest-paid professionals (race-car drivers, brain surgeons, etc.) get help putting on their work clothes. It's better to be safe than sorry.

Parents of young goalies should help their children put on the leg pads, chest protectors, and skates outside the locker room. This is because many youth coaches don't know how to resolve problems related to goalie equipment, and the locker room may be off-limits to parents or too cramped for goalies to dress comfortably. Just as forwards practice changing on the fly sometimes, a goalie and his parents may have to practice getting dressed at home a few times until they get the hang of it.

By the time a kid reaches the age 11 or 12, he should be dressing by himself (he and his coaches probably won't want parents helping out with this task anyway). The transition to self-dressing is usually gradual, but we suggest that the sooner a young goalie can dress himself, the better. This is especially true if the child plans to attend overnight hockey camp—that's not the time to learn how to don the equipment, because there won't be anyone there to help him.

Being a good net minder goes far beyond just having good technique for skating and stopping pucks. Proper preparation is required as well, both on and off the ice. We have emphasized throughout this chapter that your equipment must fit properly. Because properly fitting gear provides your body the best protection, it will improve your confidence to face shots. In fact, it's the first step in confidence building for goaltenders. With his equipment securely on, a goalie can take to the ice knowing that he has minimized the risk of physical injury—which allows him to focus completely on the job of tending the goal.

4

The Stance

The fundamental goalie stance can vary according to individual styles. However, skating ability influences how compactly the goalie moves. Hands in front, shoulders square to the action, stick on the ice (slightly angled and away from toes), head steady, knees bent, and weight on the balls of the feet—these are all components of a good ready stance. When the goalie moves from spot to spot, he should try to remain compact.

One of the game's best goalies, Dominik Hasek, provides a professional example of the ready stance. His stick is on the ice, his knees are bent, his hands are up and out, and he has total focus.

"Compact" means that the above-mentioned parts of the goalie stance *move together*—that is, the goalie moves from point A to point B while maintaining stance—and with little or no net showing through. Compact motion means that fewer parts of the goalie's body need to return to position to make the next save—and less time is wasted. Think of it this way: the goalie's hands and stick blade form a triangle that should move as a unit while the goalie is tracking. To achieve this compact motion, the goalie must see to it that his upper body moves independently of his legs.

Essentially, compactness improves economy of motion, which in turn improves speed. Of course, maintaining these essentials for compact movement depends on balance in movement, which is directly related to the goalie's ability on his skates and his leg strength. This holds for all of the goalie's actions: economy of motion actually makes the goalie faster, and compactness gives the impression of a wall moving across the net.

Instead of a six-part goalie composed of two legs, a torso, two arms, and a stick, imagine a creature in the net that is made up of six Slinkys (the springlike children's toy). If each of these Slinkys were compact, it would be easy to reposition this creature. If, however, one or more of the Slinkys are sprung, it becomes quite a chore and quite inefficient to, first, compress all the Slinkys, and, second, get the whole creature into position. The point is this: Don't be all arms and legs. Stay compact.

The Ready Stance

Moving or skating from position to position, the goalie must maintain the ready stance as much as possible. We have added the term "ready" to the conventional term "stance" because "stance" implies standing and waiting, whereas "*ready* stance" implies action—and action is central to the modern goaltender's game. From the ready stance, a goaltender can track, move to the shot lane, or pursue the puck. Historically, there are three different ready stances: the stand-up, the butterfly, and the hybrid.

Stand-Up

In this stance, the goalie stays up and rarely drops down—hence the label "stand-up." As a defining style, the stand-up ready stance is not

KID'S KEY: STANCE

- Cover the net, avoiding double coverage with your equipment.
- Be compact and in your ready stance when you move to follow the play.
- Keep your shoulders and hands steady, and skate using your legs only.

45

often a first choice anymore. It is, however, quite effective for taking away a shooter's shot lane during a straight-line challenge at the net. Coming out to the shooter and back, or telescoping (in effect, cutting down angles), is the main feature of this style.

In the stand-up ready stance, the feet are close together and the hands are between the hip and knee levels. The knees are bent, but not too much. This leaves the goalie in a more upright position than is seen in the other ready stances, with the shoulders square to the shot. The feet being close together makes tracking and puck pursuit

Stand-up ready stance: Your pads are together and closed. Maintain minimal knee bend.

more difficult, especially during lateral play-action changes. Leg saves are generally skate, two-pad, or half-split saves—which make for difficult recoveries to the ready stance.

Butterfly

The butterfly ready stance features a low crouch with the feet *more than shoulder-width* apart. The goalie's hands are out front and at about knee level. Some goalies place the trapper at either knee or shoulder height. The trapper should be in front of the body and open. Keep in mind, however, that this style covers the low part of the goal more than other styles do. So keep your hands and shoulders ready for high shots.

This stance may cause the knees to pinch, so be careful not to squeeze the knees together and lock up. Squeezing the knees may

Butterfly ready stance: Your pads are wide open and do not touch anywhere. Here you'll need maximum knee bend.

lessen the work your legs need to do to keep the stance, but it may also inhibit the quick leg movement required in many goaltending moves. Also, when the legs are locked or pinched, lateral movement is difficult; the goalie must unlock, lift, and then move laterally, which may cause him to lift his stick and lose his compact posture.

The butterfly stance is well suited for defending against lateral play-action, but it demands good leg strength. Recoveries must be quick, especially if the goalie drops early. This style puts the goalie somewhat deeper in the crease than normal (it is most effective at the edge of the crease), and often results in acrobatic and reactive moves.

A problem with goalies who use the butterfly stance exclusively is their tendency to drop down to the butterfly position on every shot, even high ones. Coaches should teach and emphasize read-and-react skills by using drills to improve butterfly decision making. They should mix high shots with low shots so that the drill does not become too predictable for the goalie.

One goalie who has mastered balancing butterfly saves with other tools is Martin Biron. Once a pure butterfly goalie, Biron has dramatically enlarged his goalie's toolbox. This has made him a far better goalie than he was when he first entered the NHL. If you favor the butterfly stance, you would do well to study Biron closely.

Hybrid

This stance is a combination of the stand-up and butterfly techniques. In other words, you use a blend of angle play and reflex/reaction to make your saves. Your feet are positioned about shoulder-width apart. This allows for fast feet in lateral play-action. With the knees bent (not pinched), the inside edges of the skates are ready to react and spring into action. The crouch is low, with the hands out in front of the body at about knee level. The trapper should be positioned at

Hybrid ready stance: Your pads touch at the top and are apart at the bottom. This way they form an upside-down V. Notice that the knee bend is moderate.

shoulder height. As with the butterfly style, some goalies prefer to start with the trapper *higher than shoulder level*. However, as the play closes in, the trapper should be gradually lowered.

Ready Stance as Defining Style

It is easy, though not always accurate, to label or stereotype a goalie according to his particular style. However, today's game has shown (and this is especially evident in the development of Dominik Hasek and Martin Biron) that a goalie must not lock into one particular style. Your ready stance will identify your starting point, but your save skills should be indifferent to your style. Getting to the shot lane and creating maximum net coverage is the number-one key to making saves. The save skill you use depends on the composition of your goalie toolbox. Everything and anything is fair game. You should use whatever tool is necessary to make the save, even if it appears to conflict with the basic style that supposedly defines you.

5

Skating

The importance of skating ability for goaltenders can't be stressed enough. Modern goaltending requires effective, active involvement in the game. The activity of goaltending goes far beyond just stopping pucks.

Surely, to make saves, the goalie needs the proper technical basics. However, a goalie who is out of position will be hard-pressed to make a save. When a goalie fields a puck behind the net or plays pucks low in the defensive zone, skating ability determines how fast the goalie gets there and back to the net. The goalie's skating skills are the basis for his ability to track play action compactly. His skates' edges get him in position for following the play action, keep him constantly in the shot lane, and maximize his ability to pursue the puck.

Active goaltending means taking charge or getting involved in the play action. Good skating is the basis for tracking the play and pursuing the puck. This can reduce the number of goal-scoring opportunities. Making saves is effectively a result of skill and positioning. The goalie's on-ice position between the puck and the net, "in the shot lane," is what makes saves possible.

Fast Feet

Too much time taken slowing down instead of stopping abruptly gives time to the shooter. Quick, direct bursts from position to position take less time than skating slow and indirect paths. Fast feet are essential to tracking the play action, minimizing setup time, and maximizing net coverage.

To gain proper position during play action, strong skating skills are absolutely necessary. Most important, the goalie's on-ice position will declare *if* the save is made. Secondarily, the goalie's save techniques and abilities declare *how* the save is made.

Skating Techniques and Related Skills

The following is a list of skating techniques and related skills that are necessary for controlled, compact movement for goalies.

1. Forward—in stance (stopping and starting): T-push/T-start; T-stop.
2. Backward (stopping and starting): T-push/C-cut; T-stop; V-stop. (*Note*: forward + backward = telescoping).
3. Lateral (side to side stopping and skating): Shuffle; T-glide (or T-push).
4. Square (gap control/*not* shrinking); compact tracking—moving laterally while keeping consistent on-ice position: in the shot

KID'S KEY: SKATING

- Move in bursts: quick stops and starts.
- Work so that both feet can do everything equally well.
- Be stopped and set just before the shot is released.

lane, shoulders at the puck; trapper and blocker and stick moving as a triangle; all for maximum net coverage.

5. Quickness and puck pursuit: get edges into ice and attack the puck.
6. Skating in general: of course, just the normal ability to skate! Inside and outside edge awareness.

Skating Exercises

The following exercises can be useful to coaches and goalies. All can be done for the length of the rink.

1. Push with left foot and glide straight with right foot (T-pushing repeat every five feet).
2. Push with left foot and glide with both feet but remain in keeper stance (repeat every five feet).
3. Push with left foot and glide with right foot, bending pushing leg so that knee nearly touches the ice.
4. Push with left foot, glide with both feet, and drop to knees and up (repeat every five or six feet).
5. Repeat 1 through 4, pushing with the right foot.
6. Run forward on the toes of skates 15 to 20 feet and then glide; repeat.
7. Skate quickly forward and jump over lines.
8. Skate forward and rotate 360 degrees on both feet at each line.
9. Skate forward and rotate 360 degrees on one foot at each line.
10. Skate forward, turn to backward skating, between blue lines.
11. Start skating backward from still, turn to forward, between blue lines.
12. Comprehensive drill—Circle Drill: Starting at the center of the circle, move (1) forward, (2) backward, (3) laterally, and (4) laterally to center. At center, always change direction as the number sequence shows. Lateral skating techniques can be selected to best reflect the goalie's skill level.

Figure 5.1 is a sample Circle Drill for a goalie with average skating ability (also see Chapter 10, "Drills"): Start at the face-off dot (in the middle). (1) T-push forward; (2) backward; (3) T-push lateral right; (4) shuffle back left; (5) backward; (6) T-push forward; (7) T-push lateral left; (8) shuffle back right.

Figure 5.1 Circle Drill

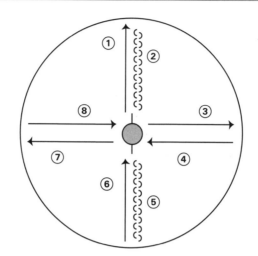

Reaction Time

Remember, however, that skating skills for the goalie should emphasize balance, traveling short distances, quick stops and starts—ultimately improving reaction time for the goalie by decreasing time and space available to shooters. Skating like a forward does is rarely done by a goalie in the course of a game. Basically, forward skating is used when fielding the puck or getting off the ice for delayed penalty calls. Goalies rely on forward, backward, and lateral skating techniques. As the player's play improves, these techniques will blend together during the course of action.

Another point—and we can't stress this enough—is that your legs must work independently of your upper body. As we discuss skating techniques, remember to be aware of your footwork and compactness. As your skating skills strengthen, your ability to carry out save skills will improve. You will gain confidence. Develop the save skills involving skating skills as well. The drills selected should allow the goalie to reach a 75 to 85 percent saves percentage by simply tracking properly and being square in the shot lane.

Forward Skating

Often young goalies seem to feel that when moving out of the net, they must skate like a forward. That's not entirely correct. Skating forward for a goalie means moving out from the net to a point in front of the net and generally just outside the crease to face a shot.

Plain and simple, a quick start and sharp stop defines skating for goalies.

T-Start

In the goalie's ready stance (get used to this phrase—it's the opener and closer for all goalie exercises), with both skates facing straight ahead, turn one skate (the pusher) 90 degrees away from the other skate (the pointer)—don't touch heels—and then push with the inside

T-push forward: Put your rear foot perpendicular to your front foot and push off with the inside edge of the rear skate to propel yourself forward.

T-push forward. While your rear foot pushes off, use your front foot to steer yourself.

edge of your pushing (sideways) skate. Remember that in the goalie stance, the knees are bent. This keeps the legs ready to push. The shoulders and goalie stick are forward and square to the shot. Coaches should keep an eye out for up-and-down, or bobbing, movement during the push forward. Do not move up and down—the push should be forward, not up. Remember: your legs should be independent of your torso.

The push has to be sharp, strong, and off the inside edge of the pushing skate ("open hip"). The pointing skate, or guide, has to be strong and steady to maintain the line or direction where you want to go. If you are less direct, that means more time for the shooter.

Young goalies will generally have trouble maintaining a straight line and should avoid bobbing up and down. To start, concentrate on the technique of the push. Your strength and precision will come with age (about 12 to 14 years old).

Generally, a goalie favors one foot to do the pushing. The goal is to become equally good pushing with either foot. If this is encouraged at an early stage, good results can be achieved sooner.

One-Skate Stop/T-Stop

As with the forward push, keep your skates independent of your upper body, and turn one skate forward so that the inside edge cuts into the ice. It's important to note that this motion can cause diffi-

One-skate T-stop: Slide your right foot forward across your body and use the inside edge of the forward skate as a brake.

culty in keeping balance. The trick is to stick out your braking skate far enough ahead to give you a larger base. This is done by turning the braking-side hip forward to get enough rotation of the skate without turning the shoulders (closed hip).

Some goalies brake with both skates—a "snow plow," like the skiers' method. This can be used for slowing down or casual movement. As mentioned before, starting and stopping must be sudden and sharp. Leave out the two-foot "snow plow" during close-in action.

Stopping with one skate, on the inside edge, is the quickest method. Remember, however, to avoid bobbing when stopping. Stay compact and keep your shoulders square to the shot. As with the T-start, learn early to stop equally well with either foot to gain an advantage in tracking. In fact, from start to stop, from making that T-start push to one-skate stop, keep the goalie's stance.

Telescoping

Aggressive goaltending means getting out there to challenge the shooter—actually, to challenge the play. That quick one-foot stop with a not-too-wide foot stance prepares the goalie for that first initial push backward.

As you well know, the play changes quickly in hockey. The goalie's quick-out to challenge may force a change in the offensive play-action. Stopping sharply enables the goalie to return or skate backward as the play approaches the net.

This alternating forward-backward movement is called telescoping. It affects proper gap control, which consists of two aspects: the relative time and space between the shooter and goalie, and also that between goalie and net. Gap control takes into account the speed of the approaching play and the relative speed of the goalie. It is really the basis for angle play. More of this later—we're getting ahead of ourselves. Let's just say that the goalie has to be between the shooter and the net so that consistently minimal net is *continuously* shown to the shooter as the play nears the net.

However, the advantage of moving out of the net to challenge the shooter is lost when the goalie's position is out of the line of the shot. The same holds true when the goalie is moving backward. Telescoping is an integral part of angle play. Proper skating technique is its basis.

Backward C-cut: The line on the ice shows the semicircle route your skate must travel to propel you backward using the inside edge of the backward-pushing skate.

Backward Skating

The backward-skating technique is directly related to the skills involved in forward skating. There is often a direct relationship between improving a goaltender's position on the ice and that goaltender's telescoping ability.

T-Push (Quick C-Cut)

The initial first push backward is similar to the T-push used in the start of the forward skate. For the backward T-push, the push-side hip is closed, or turned forward, to get the inside edge into the ice (similar to the forward stop). The push is very similar to the C-cut.

Once again, the tendency is to push upward—don't! Remember, no bobbing up and down; stay compact and always move in a prepared goalie stance.

The first T-push provides the force to get the goalie's initial backward speed up. The gliding foot serves like a ship's rudder and points *heel first* so that the goalie maintains a true line (generally in line with the near post). Sometimes, to get a proper backward thrust, two backward C-cuts (T-pushes) are good enough to get good speed and motion to the net.

Little S's

Generally, backward skating uses large, wide C strokes to get the inside edge of the skate blade to bite the ice. However, the goalie needs quick feet and readiness to react. So get onto the balls of your feet (goalies should always be on the balls of their feet when skating) and on the inside edges and make little S's on the ice. This allows you to react to any changes—forward, laterally, or diagonally.

These small quick movements have to be equal in weight, left and right side. The little S's get the inside edges to push for a short time, allowing the keeper to move backward without losing the true line or direction.

If the pushes are not equal or the initial glide of the nonpushing skate is untrue, or both occur, the goalie will drift out of the line of the shot. Keep an eye out for this drifting out of line. When skating backward, goalies tend to stare backward. Instead, it should be a quick glance—going left, look over the left shoulder; going right, look over the right. Practice with cones and slalom backward: glance and turn, look forward, and then glance.

Of course, if after the T-push there is only a small distance to cover, there is no need for the little S's. T-push with two backward pushes and then glide straight back—but keep your weight over the balls of your feet.

Backward T-Stop

Stopping is no different for backward skating than it is for forward skating. Use one skate to stop. In backward stopping, use the inside edge of one skate while maintaining the goalie stance—and stay compact! To get one skate back, the keeper has to open the stopping-side hip. "Open," of course, means turning the hip back so that the stopping skate's inside edge can bite the ice, leaving the goalie ready to go forward too. Remember that opening the hip also opens the space between the legs (that pesky "5-hole"). Try keeping the knees closer together when doing this move and keep your hands forward in the normal goalie stance. Turn only the hips and the stopping skate.

There is also the V-stop, which is used for slowing down rather than stopping. Like the forward snow plow, described earlier, the inside edges of both skates are used. But the toes are pointed outward and the heels come together, forming a "V."

The "V" technique causes difficulty in balance and foot control. It can be used in certain situations when slowing down during casual play. But generally, the one-skate technique for stopping is favored.

Backward T-stop: Your right foot goes behind your left foot. Use the inside edge of the rear (right) skate to brake your motion. In doing so, it forms a T with your other skate, which is pointing forward. Keep the skates slightly apart for balance.

We believe that one skate is the best way to stop abruptly—a skill that is needed for the fast play actions of a game.

Charging

Charging occurs when a goalie comes racing forward to stop pucks. If a shot comes at a moving goalie, it is difficult for him to move his legs—they're busy skating. Worse, if you are charging and the play moves laterally, it takes too much time to stop and turn. Consequently, our rule is this: avoid charging and racing at the shooter. Follow the game continuously with short and instant starts and stops. Be set. Move compactly, and don't waste time recuperating into your ready stance. Follow the game so that you know when and where the play action will result in a shot. *Anticipate!*

It bears repeating: the goalie's on-ice position determines if the goalie makes a save, and the goalie's style determines how he makes the save.

Lateral Movement

The play action will often move the puck from left to right and back. In these situations, lateral-skating skills are the key to properly tracking the play.

The Shuffle

This is the name for the side-to-side motion of a goalie. Sometimes the play action is a series of quick left-to-right or right-to-left slides near the front of the net. The goalie has to maintain his goalie-ready stance yet move side to side to keep his positional play, gap control, and square alignment to the action in front of the net. How to do it? Use the shuffle!

"Shuffle" seems to suggest such a slow motion for this lateral movement. But a shuffle is anything but slow. Goal-mouth scrambles are no piece of cake—the shot can come at any time. Be ready, be compact, and be in position!

The idea behind the shuffle is that the goalie covers more area of the net while maintaining his stance square to the puck. That means his shoulders, hips, toes, pads, hands, and stick are all facing the puck.

61

The shuffle does just that—and allows for lateral movement as well. The trick is to keep your skates pointed at the puck. No turning of the hips, no moving the shoulders, and most important, no twisting of the skate blades. Just keep the goalie stance and push off the inside edge of one skate and keep the other skate pointed to the puck so that the gliding skate shuffles.

Pushing off the inside edge of the skate and moving the skates without turning keeps the pads square to the puck. Remember, no bobbing up or down.

To glide or shuffle on the nonpushing skate, keep that blade flat on the ice and take some of your weight off it. This keeps your edges from biting into the ice; hence, you can shuffle.

When you want to stop (and/or return to the net), just angle the nonpushing or shuffling blade so the inside edge bites into the ice. By keeping the knees bent and staying compact, you're ready to change directions or to stop—and you are always ready to handle a shot.

Some problems occur when the goalie shuffles, opening a big space between the legs: the "5-hole." The shuffle requires quick, short

Shuffle: Here your right foot (inside edge) pushes you sideways while your left foot slides (catching no edge) lightly and flat across the ice, with the toes pointing (parallel to the pushing skate).

Shuffle with pads: Again, your right foot provides the locomotion and your left keeps you balanced.

Use your T-push lateral (left) to move across the crease and your T-push forward (right) to move out of the crease.

pushes and quick return of the pushing skate. Keep the goalie stance compact, and more important, keep the stick between the legs. This, along with fast feet, will reduce that "5-hole" space.

63

T-Push Lateral

The T-push lateral is perhaps the most commonly used move. It gives the goalie that quick push and drive to get from side to side. Like the forward T-push, the lateral T-push uses one skate's inside edge to push and the other skate to direct and glide. The difference is at the hips.

Remember that the goalie works the legs independently of the upper body. Starting in that goalie's stance and square to the play action, the pushing skate side points out and the glide skate points sideways. This opens the hip so that this skate can point to where the goalie wants to go. This forms a T shape with the skates.

The inside edge of the pushing skate bites into the ice (for the drive) and the gliding skate gives direction. The gliding skate must be surefooted and strong enough to carry the goalie's weight.

The goalie should never turn his shoulders to the direction he is moving. The shoulders, hands, and stick should stay square to the play; it's only the feet that move. Effectively, only the hip opens so that the gliding skate turns and points.

T-push lateral: To move sideways, dig your left foot's inside edge in, push off, and use your right foot as a rudder.

T-push lateral with pads: Again, your right foot leads and steers while your left foot provides the power. Keep your stick on the ice!

By keeping the knees bent, the goalie is always ready to react, be it another push or a sudden stop. Make sure there's no bobbing up and down or lifting the stick as well. There's also a tendency to let the pushing leg linger behind—a slow drag, if you will. This leaves a big 5-hole. Be sure to bring the push-side knee back quickly, just barely touching the glide-side leg. Keeping the stick square to the puck, parallel with your movement and between your skates, should help to remedy this problem.

T-Push Stopping

One hard, strong push should be enough for the goalie to get where he wants to go. To stop is rather simple. The gliding skate becomes the brake—turn it sideways and use your inside edge to bite the ice. The hip closes, turning the gliding skate around (90 degrees). Both skates should be pointing to the play action, and the goalie should be in his stance, steady and ready to react.

6

Saves and Puck Control

Skating skills are basic to effective goaltending in modern hockey. Four elements—motivation, anticipation, positioning, and equipment—are influential in any save, and all four are affected by good skating skills (see Figure 6.1). Remember that once the goalie begins to skate competently, save skills also begin to improve. Since on-ice positioning is crucial for maximum net coverage, a goalie must have superb skating skills—skating gets the goalie into the shot lane. "Where's the puck, where's the post, where am I?" should be the goalie's checkpoints.

Components of the Save

Each shot or play directed at the net should prompt a unique series of reactions on the part of the goalie. To be successful at any level, goalies must be able to track the play and pursue the puck. Skating skills get the goalie to the shot lane. Then the goalie can reach into his toolbox and use a save skill to make the save. From the chart, you can see that skating skills are the foundation for the save in all its variations.

The Goalie's Toolbox

Throughout the remainder of this book, we will occasionally touch on the concept of the goalie's toolbox. This is the notion that there are countless variations of save techniques. Beginning goalies may know, and rely on, only a few techniques to get the job done. Pro goalies will need to master up to 100 or more tools if they are to be successful.

Figure 6.1 Components of the Save

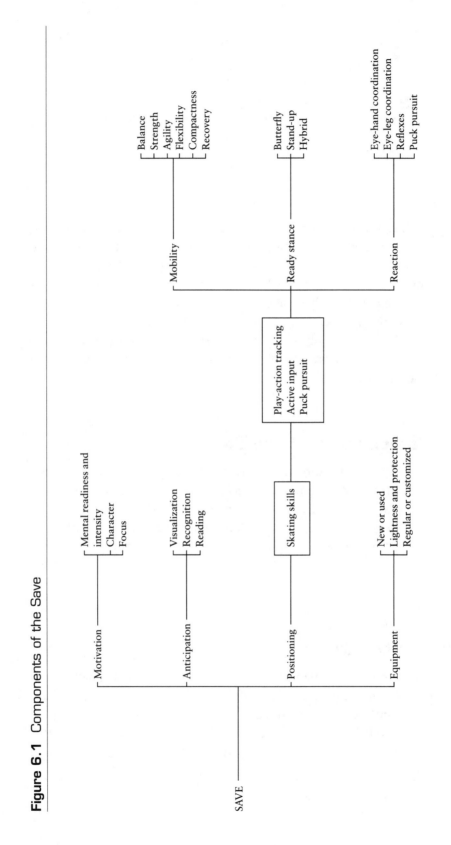

Figure 6.2 The Goalie's Toolbox

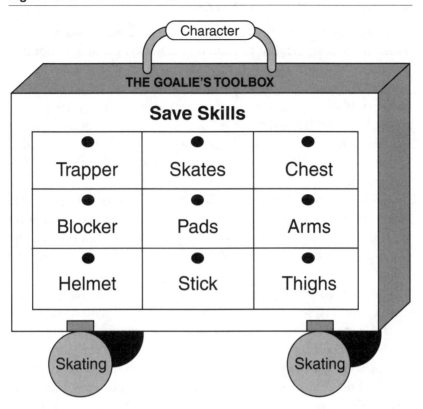

Where do you get these tools? This book should provide you with somewhere between 90 and 100 percent of the tools you'll need. To improve upon your toolbox, you'll need to become a student of the game. Read, watch, discuss, and listen to anything having to do with goaltending. Sift through it all and see what works for you.

Two things that will not change appear at the top and bottom of our toolbox: character and skating. To be a great goalie you must be committed, competitive, and respected. If your teammates see these attributes in you, they will want to battle and win for you. You must also possess superior skating skills. If you cannot skate, you won't be able to get to a shot—or recover if you happen to make the save. It is just that simple.

The nine basic save tools that should be in any goalie's toolbox will be covered in detail in this chapter. To be a great goalie, you will have to learn as many variations of these tools as possible. With experience and practice, you will then be able to call forth the right tool for the right situation.

Saves and Puck Control

Save skill refers to the skill required when reacting to make a save. There are proper methods to achieve the best coverage with optimal speed.

One challenge for younger goalies is the sheer weight of their equipment! Youth coaches should be patient: young goalies will grow stronger. For older and stronger goalies, conditioning and proper training will improve strength. But there are no shortcuts: learning save skills, especially new skills, requires patience and practice—perfect practice.

Making a save isn't merely getting in the way of or getting a piece of the puck. A lot can and does happen during the play leading up to the eventual shot on goal. Today's goaltending requires that the goalie be an active, not reactive, player. *The goalie must work the game!*

The shot-reaction-save is a result of many factors. Yet, after the save, a new situation develops. Thus, a goalie will have a direct effect on the play that follows. That's why it is not enough to simply stop pucks. The goalkeeper can have a great influence on the game—one that goes further than making saves. He faces many decisions. Steer the rebound? Freeze it? Deflect it? His decisions directly affect the flow of the game.

A save skill, therefore, has to be a complete process: skating, setting up, reaction, and so on. Review the Save Chart in this chapter once again; you will see that making a save requires a delicate balance between your skating skills and your save tools. When you are working on your save skills, remember to address the skills and tools in a balanced way so that you develop properly and completely.

A word to coaches: Your selection of drills should reflect actual game situations. Of course, this may be difficult with youth players. But you should carefully develop a long-term plan that gradually improves specific save skills and the ability to recognize gamelike situations. Of course, the plan should be based on your goalie's ability and potential.

The Skill and Its Instinctive Use

When a goalie makes a save, many factors influence his decision making and the moves he makes. To stop the shot, the goalie has to move to the proper spot and select the precise skill for dealing with that particular shot. Certain moves are dictated by the type of shot directed at the net. For example, the goaltender will instinctively move the trapper when the shot is high on the trapper side, or react with the left skate to a shot low to the left side. These instinctive reactions are the result of much practice.

10 Legitimate Criticisms You Might Hear

He goes down too early or too often.
He recovers too slowly.
He is too deep in the net.
He relies on the trapper too much.
He overhandles the puck.
He doesn't control rebounds.
He allows "soft" goals.
He doesn't anticipate well (reads and reacts poorly).
He doesn't read dekes.
He doesn't skate well.

Shots between the goalie's skills—the shot on the seam (between specific save techniques)—create the most difficulty and confusion for the goalie. These shots point up the difference between a merely adequate and a great goalie. That's why so much work must be dedicated to save skills—they must become natural reactions. We want to get you to the point where virtually no thinking is required to make a save.

Even goalies with good skills must develop the ability to make saves on the seam. In other words, they must be able to recognize and react to helter-skelter situations that arise. The distinctive factor of excellent goalkeeping is when the goaltender achieves what we like to call "compact economy of motion"—that is, he moves like a wall in the shot lane, consistently tracking the play in the line of fire, thus leaving no unnecessary holes or openings.

Solid goaltending requires work on fundamentals—the basics. Before a goaltender can expect to make—or be expected to make—the big saves, he must do a lot of work on the little things.

Save Skills Elements

Save skills can be categorized in various ways. The order chosen here considers equipment piece, its use, and recovery to stance. Remem-

Marty Biron provides a great professional example of a compact save. His stick blade is flat on the ice. His pads are placed flat along the ice and his trapper is forward on his leg pad, thus providing maximum net coverage. His eyes are following the puck all the way into his body.

ber, the complete save skill process requires the development of skills based on strong skating. For all of these techniques, compact motion is necessary. Whether at the youth or the pro level, constant diligence is required to achieve and maintain this compactness.

Every save skill requires good net awareness and use of angles. Recall how important on-ice position and skating skills are to goaltending. The recovery after an initial save is also fundamental to good goalkeeping, and will be discussed along with save skills. Controlling rebounds will be discussed in detail in Chapter 8; we will just touch on the topic in this chapter.

Before we look at the individual save tools of the goalie's toolbox, remember the key points for your initial stance and subsequent movement: Keep your head and hands steady. When you are moving, your upper body and hands should work independently of your legs. Your stance doesn't necessarily have to change; it's the overall setup that's important: Your weight should be on the balls of your feet; your knees bent and coiled; your hands in front; your stick on the ice; your shoulders over your knees and square to the puck. Your style sets up *how* you make the save; your on-ice position determines *if* you make the save.

Trapper Saves

The trapper is the glove with pizzazz. It is the one that everyone likes, since almost everyone can catch with it. Or can they? The trapper should always be kept open and facing outward. If a shot is fired and you have to open and then close the trapper, two actions occur. The first is unnecessary. Remember: economy of motion increases speed.

Keeping the glove open also provides more net coverage. The shooter sees less net, which puts pressure on him to be more accurate. It's all part of aggressive goaltending.

Some goalies like to keep the trapper with the thumb up at about shoulder level. Others like to keep it at about knee level with the

For medium-height shots, catch the puck in your trapper while utilizing a half-butterfly, straight-leg action.

thumb out. Both are correct, as along as your technique fits with your overall basic stance. Hasek, Biron, Noronen, and Roloson are excellent examples of goalies who correctly use the thumb-up technique with the thumb-out technique as the play action nears.

Using the trapper

- Keep the glove steady! Don't move your trapper around when your legs are moving.
- Follow the puck all the way into the trapper with your eyes.

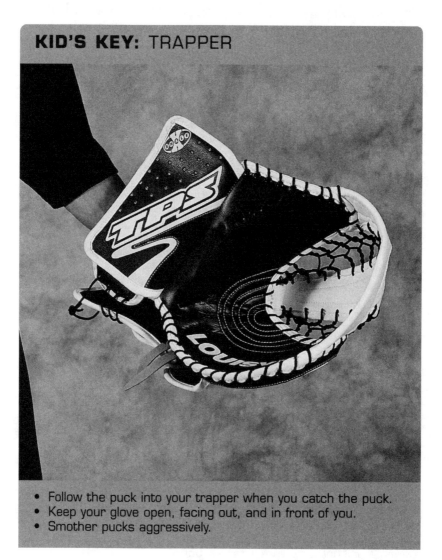

KID'S KEY: TRAPPER

- Follow the puck into your trapper when you catch the puck.
- Keep your glove open, facing out, and in front of you.
- Smother pucks aggressively.

- Keep your head steady so the puck doesn't seem to move up and down. (Think of how a falcon's head doesn't bob up and down as it watches its prey.) To achieve this, the legs must move independently of the upper body. When your head is steady, eye-hand coordination is easier to achieve, and you can get a better read on the puck.
- Catch the puck with the *whole* glove. Some goalies try to catch with just the tip of the webbing—don't! Remember to put as much as possible *behind* the puck. The whole glove is more than just the webbing. Eye the puck all the way into the middle of the basket.
- Keep your hands in front and avoid double coverage—placing the trapper in front of your chest protector or in front of your pad while in the ready stance. Allow for free movement of

It's all about puck protection. You should always try to create multiple barriers so your opponents can't get at the puck and the puck can't get past you. Here, the blocker and stick are placed in front of the puck, the trapper is placed over the puck while pushing down, and the pads are behind the puck (and the other equipment we just mentioned).

your trapper. Keep the trapper open; close it only when a puck enters it!

- Long shots or shots that give you time should be backed up. Get your body or your blocker behind the puck. The shot is often straight and true, but deflections and drops are the order of business during a game. The goalie must play the shot expecting any eventuality—that's anticipation!

KID'S KEY: BLOCKER

- Deflect or angle pucks away from trouble with your blocker.
- Become just as good with your blocker as you are with your trapper.
- When you smother pucks, put your blocker in front of your trapper for protection.

- Do not use the trapper like a blocker. We've seen goalies who are content merely to let the puck hit their trapper, which often leads to a dangerous rebound. Catch the puck!
- When covering up pucks on the ice, push down with your trapper as if you want to push the puck through the ice. Protect the puck by putting your blocker and stick in front of your trapper. Anticipate! You never know when an opponent will try to jar the puck loose.

Use your blocker to angle shots away from the net. You don't need to lurch forward with the blocker. Merely turn it slightly and let the momentum of the puck work for you.

In general, the trapper is used for shots from just below the knee to the top corner of the net. The trapper is an excellent piece of equipment; it can stop pucks and stop the play in one motion. However, don't overuse it.

Blocker Saves

The blocker glove connects to two pieces of equipment: the blocker and the goalie stick. These two tools should work together, and they certainly should not interfere with each other. The blocker is generally used to deflect pucks that are between the knee and shoulder level (the top shelf of the net)—on the stick side, of course.

Deflecting Pucks Away. The blocker is positioned (like the trapper) slightly ahead of the knees. When shots are directed to the blocker side, it is enough to *angle* the blocker in the direction you want it to go. You don't necessarily have to lurch it forward. The force of the shot will carry the puck away.

Aggressive goaltending means taking charge of situations. A bad rebound is another scoring chance! When possible, deflect the puck away from the traffic in front of the net. Don't be content to let the puck just hit your blocker. If you don't redirect the puck away, more often than not it will drop into a prime scoring region.

At youth levels of play, deflecting pucks to the blocker-side corner is good enough. Advanced goalies may actually try to deflect the puck by passing it to their teammate—now, *that's* active goaltending! This takes a lot of practice.

Like the trapper, keep the blocker hand steady, especially when moving in the net area. There are two reasons for this. First, it improves eye-hand coordination; second, the blocker movement directly influences the goalie stick.

Holding the Stick. The blocker hand should hold the goalie stick in trigger fashion (see the "Stick Saves" section later in this chapter), with the index finger extended down the paddle. Here's a tip for goalies having problems with the stick not staying on the ice: do not choke the stick; rather, push the hand down onto the paddle section so that whatever movement occurs, the stick will remain on the ice. This technique takes time. But when it works properly, the shoulder, elbow, wrist, and blocker hand work together and the stick just follows.

You can use the blocker and trapper together. Pin the puck on top of your blocker using your trapper (left), or form a basket by bringing both your blocker and your trapper together (right).

During the blocker save, try to get as much of you (and as many pieces of equipment) behind the puck as possible—anticipate the worst-case scenario.

Blocker/Trapper Combination Saves

When tracking play, think of your two hands and the blade of your stick as forming a triangle; the three should move together. Your two gloves should work together, especially when it comes to rebound control. This skill takes good coordination and timing. As the shot arrives, the goalie's blocker should be angled down and turned slightly into the body. Then the trapper is brought across the belly with the trapper thumb pointed upward and outward. Bring the two gloves together and use the trapper to pin the puck onto the top of the blocker. For low (5-hole or chest) shots, bring your hands together to cradle the puck off your body in a basket fashion. Don't forget one of our essential rules: Get as much behind the puck as you can. Whenever possible, get your torso behind your gloves. That way, the puck has to penetrate multiple barriers in order to get past you.

If you have time, you may want to reach across your body and use your trapper to catch the puck on your blocker side. You are less likely to create a rebound this way.

Generally, shots occur so fast that there is no time to plan these save skills. Yet, when time permits, using your trapper and blocker together is an excellent way to control the game. Freeze the puck, drop the puck, pass the puck—all of these actions constitute active input. You work the game; don't let it work you.

Catching on the Blocker Side. Sometimes it may be possible to catch the puck with the trapper on the blocker side. Generally, a goalie can use this technique on long shots or other shots that give him time to perform this skill.

First, get the blocker up and angled to make the save. If time permits, bring the trapper across the front of your chest to the front of the blocker. Now make a backhanded catch with the trapper. Here's a trick: Recall that the trapper thumb is pointed up or out, depending on the goalie's preference in the ready stance. To catch the puck on the blocker side, roll the trapper hand in a semicircle so that the trapper thumb arrives at the blocker with the thumb pointed *down*. This way the trapper is ready to catch. The blocker is angled and ready just in case the trapper doesn't get there in time! Try this right where you are sitting. Easy, isn't it? This skill, and most glove-save skills, are readily practiced off-ice. Practice these motions using your gloves and have a friend toss a tennis ball, puck, or sponge puck.

Ideally, you will be able to use the most protected areas of your arms—your hands—when making saves. Sometimes, a shot hand-cuffs the goalie. In this case, the goalie must use his arm to make the save. In fact, there may be times when you will be able to get only a shoulder, biceps, or forearm in front of the puck. There are two neg-atives associated with such saves. First, rebounds off these body parts are difficult to direct or control. Try, when possible, to angle the puck away from you and away from the front of the net. Second, shots to these areas may sting because your padding is not as thick and leaves coverage gaps.

If it is a choice between getting scored on and feeling a shot, win-ning goalies will choose the save, even if it comes with a welt. This is the price you will have to pay sometimes; getting dinged up is part of the game. If, however, these stings are too severe and too frequent, you may need new equipment with better padding in these areas.

Keep your skate blade flat on the ice and use it to deflect the puck into the corner and out of danger.

Chest Saves

As discussed previously, the simplest technique here is to merely allow the puck to hit your chest pad and then cradle the puck to your body using your trapper and/or blocker. This tool is especially effective when it is combined with the butterfly save.

If you cannot cradle the puck, try to deaden it and pounce on it after it falls to the ice. The skill requires a square ready stance with shoulders at the puck during the chest save. This positions the chest angled downward; the puck then deflects down.

Skate Saves

Today's game is getting faster and faster, and goalies need to react more and more quickly; consequently, the skate save is not often seen, and is seldom taught, anymore. Indeed, some of our peers will tell you to never consider this tool. However, we believe that when the occasion presents itself, you should know how to use it—properly.

The half-split, or skate, save is a good technique on long shots that the goalie wants to deflect away from traffic. The main drawback associated with this technique is the big space it leaves between the legs—the dreaded 5-hole! But done at a key time, it's excellent for rebound control. The kicking blade is angled and extended, deflecting the puck into the corner. However, be aware that there's a good chance you'll be off balance after this sequence of moves. Quickness in recovery to stance is important.

Here's how it's done: From the goalie stance, the reacting or kicking skate turns in a way that inscribes a small arc on the ice. The skate blade remains flat on the ice at all times. The arcing motion finishes with the skate blade angled away from the play action and toward the corner. The blade travels and comes to rest on its outside edge. Note that this method is the same for either foot, and it can often involve the stick in combination with the skate.

To get this motion of the arc and to get onto the outside edge of the saving skate, your hip on the side the puck is shot to must open—that is, the hip must turn to the outside. This allows your leg to turn so that the outside edge of the blade is flat on the ice for full coverage by the blade. On the blocker side, avoid moving your stick blade past the kicking skate blade.

As you kick your one leg out for the half-split or skate save, your other leg simultaneously drops, in a compact manner, to your knee on the other leg. Initially, you may have a tendency to sit. But goalies should bend down—not fall down.

It's very important that your shoulders stay square to the initial shot. Often, the tendency is to turn the shoulders and skate toward the puck. Younger goalies frequently have this problem. This save requires quick feet to get in front of the puck. Trying to skate there and make the save at the same time takes too long. Remember, especially for leg saves, that the hips and legs work independently of the hands and upper body. Keep your shoulders up and square to the action.

Skate and Stick Combination Saves

For shots on the trapper side, slide your stick along the ice to give yourself more puck coverage. Avoid over-rotating with your stick-hand shoulder. The stick, like the skate, should be angled. The force of the puck hitting the stick or skate will deflect the puck out of harm's way, effectively controlling the rebound. The trapper follows the leg action and remains open, providing maximum net coverage.

For shots on the blocker side, the skate save is even more of a skate save than the glove side. Owing to the shape of your stick and the directon the blade is pointing, it's pretty obvious that you cannot have the stick go through the same range of motion. Here, you will lead with the heel of your stick. As a rule, keep the stick on the ice and *don't* move the heel of the goalie stick beyond the heel of your skate.

The optimal technique for the skate save depends on independent legwork, good stick-hand coordination, and square upright shoulders. You can't be skating or drifting when trying to make the save.

To recover from the skate save, retrace the arc traveled by the kicking skate to its original point beneath your body. Once that skate is under you, bite into the ice with the *inside edge* of the blade and push up. This is the one-leg recovery to the goalie stance.

Of course, the strength of the goalie's legs (especially the quadriceps, or thigh muscles) and glutes (fanny muscles) varies with age. Balance and strength will increase over time. Be patient while you develop this technique and your strength. Check out the pictures in the next section to see how your stick should move in conjunction with your leg.

Leg Saves

Leg saves are perhaps the most difficult to perfect. You tend to "stand" on your legs. That's the good news, but it's also the bad

KID'S KEY: LEG PADS

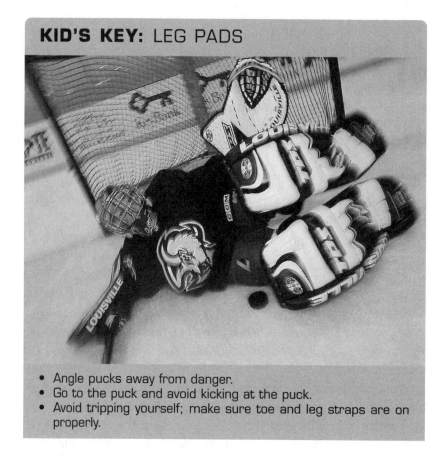

- Angle pucks away from danger.
- Go to the puck and avoid kicking at the puck.
- Avoid tripping yourself; make sure toe and leg straps are on properly.

news. You can't just stand stiff on your legs; they should feel like springs, with knees unlocked and cocked to react. We encourage those who are training off-ice to skip rope and perform plyometrics—they develop lightness and agility for the feet. Agility and balance games with a soccer ball are excellent off-ice ways to improve eye-leg coordination and leg agility.

Many shots are directed at the bottom half of the net. So a lot of work must be dedicated to leg saves. Actually, legwork is what makes the difference between good goaltending and great goaltending. Your legs get you where you want to be (reaction), control your agility (compactness), affect your positioning (tracking), and make a large percentage of saves.

Let's look at the common themes for every type of leg save. Remember that much of our discussion of leg saves applies to the skate and the various pad saves.

Those big "pillows" tend to create big rebounds. Controlling these rebounds is difficult. To make the initial save is a big enough challenge. Shots on goal between the knee and the ice sometimes cause indecision. Do I catch the puck? Do I kick out? These "lower-half" shots cause problems for save-skill decisions, save-skill executions, and rebound control. This is why the development of this skill requires practice and patience, both on and off the ice.

On the ice you want compact movement and decisive actions. Pad or leg saves involve all parts of the body: the head, the shoulders, the hands, and, yes, the legs too. How the goalie initially sets up and how the goalie reacts have a direct effect on his ability to stop the puck and recover. Ideally, move to the puck and avoid kicking at the puck.

It is important that your shoulders and hands react compactly. Both should move toward the oncoming puck. Balance is the key. The shoulders should not be too far forward or too far back. As a coach, you can determine this by watching from the side as your goalie makes saves. Does the goalie "lift"? Does an uncontrolled fall happen after making a leg save? How difficult is it for the goalie to get back into his ready stance?

The best level of play is achieved when the legs and hips work independently of the hands and shoulders—the legs making the save as the shoulders and hands move toward the puck. This will maintain balance and help in recoveries to stance. Yet all must work together. You must be compact and square to the play.

Half-Butterfly Saves. For the game as we see it today, the "half butterfly" is perhaps the most effective low-shot save technique. With proper execution and position, this save skill can cover virtually the whole bottom half of the net.

What coaches should watch for and goalies should avoid is dropping down to the half butterfly just for the sake of it. The half butterfly is an effective technique, but it is not the only technique. Keep an eye out for this at all levels. During play, decision making is as important as reacting. Merely dropping down is different from making low-shot saves.

The technique is an excellent tool because a large number of shots are directed at the bottom half of the net. Compared with the skate save, the half butterfly covers the 5-hole much more effectively.

The basic method (for either the trapper side or stick side) starts much like that of the skate save: shoulders are upright and square to the play, hands are in front, and movements are compact. Bring one knee to the ice and simultaneously kick out the other leg toward the puck. This leg, the save leg, is extended so that the skate's toe faces forward; this allows the whole pad to face forward.

There are two types of half-butterfly save:

Use a half-butterfly save with your leg flush to the ice to stop pucks shot along the ice or with traffic in front.

Use a half-butterfly save with your leg straight for toe saves and high shots.

Pad flush to the ice. The difficulty of this leg movement is overcome by pointing your save-side hip forward—that is, closing the hip (contrary to the skate save's open-hip technique).

Straight-legged. This is the alternative to the skate, or half-split, save. Simply extend the save leg straight sideways and follow with your stick. This technique will, of course, leave a small gap between your pad and the ice.

For either half-butterfly type, on shots to the trapper side, the trapper extends over the save pad. Sometimes a goalie will follow with the stick. For rebound control, the stick can be used to deflect the puck away from the play. The goalie must decide whether a deflection or a rebound is the greater threat.

The goalie's decision making will improve with experience, as will his use of his stick. If you notice too many 5-hole goals, the technique has not yet been perfected.

For shots to the blocker side, your stick's heel should pass the extended leg (like the half split). The blocker hand extends over the blocker-side pad. When extending the blocker hand, remember to keep your stick on the ice. This may be difficult, but good articulation of the wrist, elbow, and shoulders will provide you with the proper extension.

Taking the half butterfly to another level, the kneeling leg can be slid in behind the save leg upon impact. This way, the small 5-hole (which cannot be avoided with this technique) is now covered. This move covers the whole bottom half of the net, just like a wall. It is especially effective when dealing with traffic in front of the net—everything from deflections to scrambles.

Active and aggressive goaltenders are involved in the play. It's not enough to just save the puck; great goalies make saves on the play. For instance, you can anticipate deflections by following the play, reading the action, and using a half-butterfly save skill with traffic in front on a shot that looks wide. Anticipation means reading all options.

For recovery to the ready stance, bring the save leg back under your body. As with the skate-save recovery, bite into the ice with your inside edge to push yourself up and back onto your feet.

Recovery to goalie stance is directly affected by the save-skill execution. The half-butterfly recovery requires that during the save you keep your shoulders upright and square to the play. Remember, as always, that the upper body should be independent of the legs. Pop up forcefully. Strength varies from person to person: if you place your hands on the ice to steady yourself, this means your head and shoulders are too far forward or backward. They should be upright and square to the play.

Full-Butterfly Saves. The butterfly is the skill that defines the butterfly goalie. The butterfly save, like the others we've talked about, is an important tool in the goalie's toolbox. It is especially effective for shots fired directly at your legs or at the 5-hole. It also maximizes net

Use the classic butterfly save to stop shots with your outstretched pads and upright torso. Keep your hands up.

coverage on close-range play action. The butterfly skill can also be used to stop big rebounds off the pads. Other excellent uses of the butterfly save are for center-screen shots and deflections in traffic.

Since screens are created when players of both teams converge in front of the net, the goalie must concentrate on protecting the area of least coverage. The upper bodies of the players cover most of the upper part of the net (upper bodies cover more space than legs). The screen shot has a greater chance of getting through the forest of legs (area of least coverage). Here, using the butterfly (and half butterfly, for that matter) gives good net coverage.

Frankly, many goalies use this technique at the wrong time. The butterfly skill is not a license to drop to your knees. When game situations such as screens, deflections, and rebounds develop, your decision making should guide your use of the butterfly. Otherwise, stay on your feet! Marty Biron uses the best blend of butterfly skills and other skills to enhance his toolbox of saves.

There are two variations of the full-butterfly save:

Butterfly classic. Starting from the ready stance, the butterfly save skill requires good compact movement. As the knees go down to the ice, your feet move outward to form a "V" shape covering more low net area. Keep the hands ready and up. Your shoulders should be square and upright, with your hands out in front. The classic butterfly save, done at its very best, has the leg pads extended out to both sides and the skate blades running as parallel as possible to the ice. This gives full exposure of the pads to the shot. It is very important that your knees stay close together from the beginning of your downward movement to your final save position—the 5-hole must be blocked.

Your trapper should be extended out and open, and your blocker hand should maintain the flexibility and position needed to keep the stick on the ice and in front. However, for central shots and rebound control, you should react with your hands out in front and closing on the puck.

If you are using the butterfly save and rebounds are coming off your torso and thighs too often, that means your hands are late. Many 5-hole goals from screens and long shots occur because the goalie's knees aren't touching, the hands are late, the stick is off the ice, or the legs are slow because the knees are locked from the initial ready stance.

High-shot goals can be a problem, because the butterfly save brings the goalie to his knees. For younger goalies whose opponents can't raise the puck, there is always a temptation to over-rely on this save technique. In fact, sometimes the coach has to *unteach* going down.

Remember to keep your edges in the ice as much as possible. Tracking and puck pursuit are difficult from the knees.

Butterfly block. Basically, the butterfly block gives very good net coverage on low shots, screens, deflections, and in tight lateral play-action. As with the butterfly classic, your knees are down and your feet are extended out. The difference is the position of your hands: your blocker and trapper move down to the tops of the pads. Note how the stick is extended forward and angled. Don't worry—the puck will deflect into your body. Having your hands at your sides and your legs in the butterfly make for a very large blocking area. Beware of your hands lagging up, and remember to have good gap with the shooter. All butterfly skills are more effective at the top of the crease or higher.

Recovery to the goalie stance from both the butterfly classic and butterfly block can be accomplished in one of two ways: the direct-lift method uses a pushing and jumping-up action to get you off your knees. Once the lift has provided sufficient clearance under you, slide your skates in and under you to get onto the inside edges of both blades. This skill may be difficult for youngsters who haven't developed enough leg strength.

Use the butterfly block to give you maximum coverage when facing low shots, screens, and deflections. Here, you lower your hands to your sides and position them just above your pads.

The one-leg recovery method uses the inside edge of one skate. As with the half-butterfly and skate save, one knee is lifted so that the skate's edge can bite. This push upward gives clearance for the other knee to lift and get its skate's edge into the ice. The method is basically a two-step lift. You may naturally favor one leg, but try to become good at using both.

When it's necessary to recover *and* move laterally, you should use the one-leg method instead of a direct lift so that the first skate can push off and move you laterally as you get back onto your feet and into the shot lane of the next play action.

Pad Saves

Most shots are directed at the bottom half of the net. Not surprisingly, the pads are used to stop most shots from the knee to the ice. The goalie's pads are very busy.

The goalie must be ready to react to any situation—there's very little time to think. Many coaches refer to this as "read and react." We think there is a third step, especially for goalies: goalies must read, *interpret*, and react.

Try to make the save with no rebound—or, at the least, with a rebound that is angled, or deflected away from the action in front of

You will use the angled-pad save numerous times over the course of a game. All you need is a slight angle to redirect the puck away from the net. Until you are more experienced at kicking rebounds in a certain direction, just let the pad and momentum of the puck do the work.

the net. At the top levels of play, a goalie is like an inverted letter "V," deflecting pucks to the sides. Admittedly, doing this with pad saves is very difficult.

Deflection Technique. The deflection method redirects the force of the shot and puts the puck out of harm's way. The pads are slightly angled in a manner to deflect the puck (be careful not to turn sideways). Sometimes, the goalie can actually push or even kick back at the puck so that the puck deflects back almost as hard as it arrived. This is a more advanced technique, requiring excellent timing and decision making. It is very effective for getting the puck away from the net safely.

"Deaden" technique. The "deaden" method is exactly what the term implies: the pads absorb the shock of the puck, deadening any rebound. This method requires very good motor skills and leg control. It must also provide the goalie sufficient time to cover the loose

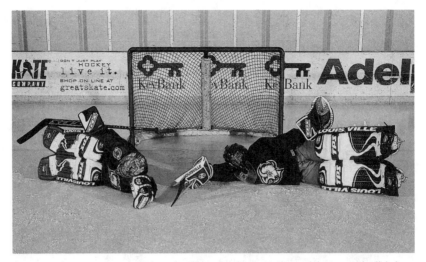

Among the most sensational saves is the stack pad (two-pad slide). Purposefully use any and all other pieces of your equipment (stick, arms, gloves) to obtain maximum net coverage.

puck. If this skill is not done properly, the puck will just lie on the ice, where an opposing player can knock it into the net.

The shock is absorbed by softening the save leg. Just as a player receives a pass with his stick and deadens the shock, the goalie should make his pads "give" to absorb the puck. But first, you need to get your pad into the puck/shot lane. Avoid kicking *at* the puck. Kicking out at the puck will stop it, but it also is likely to create a rebound that goes right back to the shooter's stick. Ideally, you fully absorb the shot or you angle your pad to deflect the puck away from the net. Thus, rebounds are either nonexistent or controlled.

Remember that, for all leg-pad saves, the hands and stick should move at the puck as well. This helps with rebound control and ensures maximum net coverage.

Stack-Pad Saves

Generally, the two-pad save can be used for close-in lateral passing plays leading to a shot. It can also be used for a diagonal move to defend against a breakaway shot. When the shooter elects to deke laterally and tries to move around you, stack the pads to that side.

A critical decision is whether to leave your feet: Should I throw myself? Should I stay on my feet because it's not time? Leaving your feet to get in the way of the puck should be a last resort, because it will not permit you to pursue the puck with recovery and quickness.

The stack save, like the half-butterfly and butterfly saves, requires goalies to react and move their ready stance downward, but it is *not* a license to drop down onto the ice. Stacking is a good skill, but it should not be used very often—too many stack saves usually means that the goalie's decision making is faulty and leads others to label him a "flopper." This technique uses strong thrusts from the shuffle or T-push for the initial lateral movement. The slide, or end result, is a T-glide with the stacking of the pads into the shot lane or tight at the puck.

Recall from our discussion of the T-push that the pointing skate is the directional skate. When executing a stack-pad save, the move is not really lateral—it's diagonal. You must open your hip more than usual for a stack save. To simplify our discussion, the technique will be described as a move going from the right to the left.

From the initial goalie stance, the right skate's inside edge gives the first push. At the same time, the pointing (left) skate is aimed in the direction you want to go. The knee of this pointing skate (in this case, the left skate) must be bent deeply and the hip must be open. This initial thrust resembles a T-push.

After the main push, the right leg swings *behind* and under the left-pointing leg. The outside edge of the pushing leg (right) slides along the ice, lifting the left pad. The bottom leg must be fully extended. The action causes the pads to stack—in this case, left on top of right. Picture it this way: you are running from first to second base, and you slide into second on your side.

In the final position the upper body is slightly bent at the hips, bringing the shoulders toward the puck. Thus, your body will resemble a very shallow "V." This gives you more control by preventing any rolling backward or forward.

Sliding toward the glove side: The trapper is kept open and placed on top of the hip. The stick and blocker may be extended out into the slot (to intercept deflections, rebounds, or passes) or placed square along the ice in front of the belly and pants to plug any holes underneath and provide an additional barrier.

Sliding toward the blocker side: The trapper arm is generally extended out into the slot. The stick is placed along the length of the top pad in the stack.

There are some differences of opinion when it comes to recovery from this stack-pad save. Depending on the goalie's level and age and on the game situation, the recovery method will vary. There are two simple rules that apply to all recoveries: (1) always face the puck and play, and (2) use the fastest method.

Push-up recovery: Here, two arms and both legs are used. The hips are rolled forward so the hands and knees are set up on all fours. Note that this violates one of our rules: keeping your body square to the play. At best, keep your eyes on the puck. This method is generally used at youth levels where strength influences how well skills are performed.

Two-point recovery: This method is technically sound but requires more skill and strength. It's a one-arm/one-leg technique. The arm along the ice pushes up, lifting the shoulders and hips. Simultaneously, the leg along the ice is brought back under the body. This clears the way for the top leg's skate to get its *inside edge* to bite into the ice—hence the "one arm, one leg." In our previous example, the right arm and left leg would be the levers used to right yourself. Pushing off the opposite skate allows more clearance for the ice-side pad to recover, as in the half butterfly. Furthermore, this is a recovery with square shoulders, and freedom of movement for you to maximize your next action.

A final note: Some problems occur when the two-pad stack skills are not properly executed. First, you can have bouncing on the hips and the puck slides under you. Second, the shoulders (after coming in contact with the ice) may not be square to the action. Here, if your back arches forward too much, you will be on your belly after the slide. If your back arches backward, you will end up flat on your back after the slide. In either case, recovery is difficult and net coverage is difficult.

A balanced stack-pad save is the result of proper execution. Errors in technique will lead to a noncompact motion. Coaches should check the goalie's skating skill during lateral movement and look carefully at the leading or pointing skate leg: for fit it should be bent deeply.

Knee/Thigh Saves

Like saves with your arms, saves on shots that are thigh-high rely on secondary options. These saves are made with the equipment covering your thighs (pants, knee guard, and cup). Naturally, you would

KID'S KEY: STICK

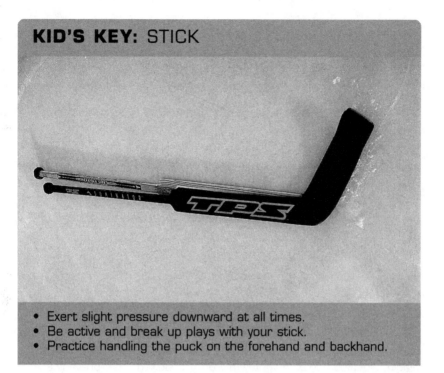

- Exert slight pressure downward at all times.
- Be active and break up plays with your stick.
- Practice handling the puck on the forehand and backhand.

Firmly grip the stick at the top of the paddle. If your grip is too hard, your hand will tire. If your grip is too loose, pucks will spin or turn your stick. Separate and extend your index finger down the paddle as your thumb and other three fingers grip the stick for better control.

When making a stick save, if you cushion the puck by angling and placing your stick blade slightly in front of you, you can prevent a rebound.

prefer to use your leg pads, because they are more nimble and offer greater protection. But you should learn to keep your skates on the ice and not lift. Also, you should first try to get your hands at the puck, either to make the save or control the rebound.

As is the case with shots that strike you in the arm, pucks that hit you in the pants or knee are more likely to generate unpredictable rebounds. Thigh-high shots may also find their way to unprotected or underprotected areas. These could sting. If possible, play through the pain and seek help when the next whistle blows.

Stick Saves

If you ask most young goalies "Why do you have a stick?" their answer often will be "To shoot the puck better." This is not entirely correct. Active goaltending certainly requires stick-handling skills. However, the real reason for the stick is to stop pucks along the ice. A curved stick definitely helps you lift and flip the puck. However, curved sticks can be disadvantageous in at least three situations: when going to the backhand; when the goalie catches left-handed but naturally shoots right-handed or vice versa; and when keeping the blade completely flat on the ice. For these situations, a shallower curve or straight stick may be the solution.

The stick is gripped at the joint where the shaft and the paddle (sometimes referred to as the "built-up" section) meet. The index finger generally cradles the paddle, while the thumb and other three fingers grip the shaft. The stick hand should be pushing the stick blade down into the ice. We recommend building a knob on the end of the stick so that it will not easily slide out of your hands or, if necessary, it can be easily picked up if dropped. These days, there is lightweight tape and foam ends, so these knobs need not affect the feel of the stick, as was once the case.

Stick Control. To lessen the impact of a shot, push down on the stick's paddle section and place your stick 6 to 12 inches in front of your feet. It is important that your stick be angled slightly back toward you, because the puck's force will drive the bottom part of the blade backward. The proper distance, angling, and downward pressure help you absorb the shot—and prevent a rebound.

Active goaltending means involvement in the play. In the event of a rebound, be ready to react—a loose puck lying in front of the goal leads to much traffic. Opposing players will do whatever it takes to get the puck past you. To deflect the puck away from danger, you must be able to control the rebound. Stick control facilitates rebound control.

On-Ice, Low Shots. Low shots often must be deflected away from traffic. Sometimes (usually at more advanced levels of play), the redirection can be to a teammate—that's excellent rebound control. This can be a definite advantage—for example, if you can, with one action that combines a save and a pass, start an offensive breakout from your defensive zone. Often these low saves rely on a combination of stick and leg saves. When using such a combination save, be sure to avoid the "can opener"—rapidly snapping the stick-hand wrist, which lifts the blade off the ice and allows the puck to slide under the stick. Keep your hands and stick facing the puck and position the pad to back up the angled stick.

Half-Split Stick Saves. The method used in these saves actually uses the shot's speed and power to your advantage. Point the toe of the skate out and butt it up against the stick. Simultaneously, arch your stick-side shoulder (keeping stick flush to the ice) in the direc-

For pucks coming from behind the net on your blocker side, hold your ground next to the post and use a short poke check to disrupt the play or deflect a pass.

For pucks coming from behind the net on your trapper side, hold your ground next to the post and use a short poke check to disrupt the play or deflect a pass.

This close-up illustrates the importance of at-post skate positioning. It is the only way for you to prevent pucks from sneaking through. These can be very embarrassing goals.

tion you want the puck to go. The stick efficiently angles the puck to the side. See the earlier section "Skate Saves," too, as these two saves can be used together.

Some goalies kick the stick to try to push the puck away faster. At the pro level, this is usually done to speed up the rebound, making it more difficult for opponents to handle. Youth and other less-experienced goalies must be careful, however, because this move may result in a fan on the shot and a goal for the opposition—which can be very embarrassing.

As we pointed out, the force of the shot against an angled stick will send the puck out of harm's way. On the other hand, kicking tends to lift the stick, and that's very dangerous if it is not timed properly. Master the initial technique first; then work on speeding up the rebound.

Half-Butterfly Stick Saves. With the basic half-butterfly leg save, the stick also moves at the puck. By angling the stick, the goalie uses the force of the shot to deflect the puck away. This method allows for more net coverage. The half-butterfly relies on either the whole leg pad or the stick (with the pad behind it) to make the save. Hence, 5-hole coverage is vastly improved (see "Half-Butterfly Saves" and the accompanying photo earlier in this chapter).

Full-Butterfly Stick Saves. This save follows the same principles as the half-butterfly stick save. Be sure to keep your hands ahead of you. This allows the stick to pursue the puck as you turn your shoulders in its direction. Go back to the "Leg Saves" section to see photos of how the leg, skate, and stick work together.

Stick Checks

Stick checks are aggressive moves that take time and space—or the puck itself—away from the shooter. When there's no puck, of course, there is no shot. The essence of active goaltending is trying to control the play through aggressive actions. Stick checks are especially effective when the play involves passes through the crease area and wraparounds. The following stick-check tools should be of help, depending on the situation. However, as with all goaltending skills, you must learn which ones to pull out of your toolbox—and when—so that you can solve the problems you are faced with.

Short Poke Check

With the short poke check, the goalie uses the blade of his stick to strip an opponent of the puck or otherwise hinder the opponent's progress. Typically, the goalie takes up a stance on either post when the puck is in the corner, or to the side of or behind the net. His arm is extended slightly, but his hand stays where the shaft and paddle meet. This check is especially useful for clearing loose pucks in and around the crease.

To execute this check properly, make sure of the following:

- Only the heel of your skate and your rear end are in the net.
- Your pads are outside the net and your puck-side pad is up against the post.
- Your hands are ahead of your body.
- Your shoulders are facing outward, to the front of the net as much as possible, with your puck-side hands, elbows, and shoulders outside of, and wrapped around, the post.
- Your stick blade is on the ice, beyond your post-side toe, square to the passing lane and just off the post.
- Your head is on a swivel; this allows you to anticipate where the threat is should the pass get through, see off-puck players, and focus on the puck.

Your active input as the goalie is to force a "saucer," or poor pass. But, if the puck gets through, you must be able get to the shot lane using your puck-pursuit and tracking skills.

It's important that you *never place the stick's blade inside* the toe of the post-side skate. If you do, there is a risk that the puck will deflect off the stick, between your skates, and—ugh!—into the goal.

Here's a good technique for strengthening a hold on the post with the post-side skate: As the skate approaches the post, angle the calf and ankle away from the post. When the blade touches the post, return the leg to its upright position. This move gets the inside edge of the skate blade into the ice without leaving the post. The more someone tries to jam at the skate, the more the blade's inside edge bites into the ice, making it harder to move. Your other leg must always be ready to move out, across, or to make a save.

Long Poke Check

The long poke check is an aggressive move that a goalie executes by rapidly sliding his hand from the paddle to the knob of his stick, then

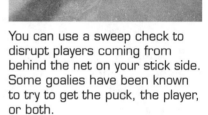

You can use a long poke check to challenge an oncoming shooter. This is a high-risk, high-reward play. You must make a commitment to go, yet wait as long as possible to fire the stick out, which maximizes the surprise factor.

You can use a sweep check to disrupt players coming from behind the net on your stick side. Some goalies have been known to try to get the puck, the player, or both.

101

using the full length of the stick and his arm to separate the puck from an opposing player's stick. If a goalie can do this speedily, he can hide his intentions. The goalie keeps his blade on the ice and throws it at the stick of the puck carrier. The knob of the goalie's stick should jam in the hand so there is no possibility of losing the stick. This check is quite effective in thwarting breakaways, in tight action, and for clearing loose pucks. However, if done improperly, it can leave the goalie off balance and out of position. Although this check is not used often, it's a valuable tool.

When defending against a breakaway, the goalie should never simply stop in his tracks and lunge forward with a long poke check. Rather, he should execute the check while continuing to skate backward and maintaining gap control. There are two reasons for this: (1) the element of surprise is enhanced; and (2) if you miss, you're still in the way. After the long poke check, remember to quickly return to your ready stance and position the stick for the next play action.

Sweep Check

The sweep check is an active goaltending maneuver that places the full length of the stick flush to the ice like a windshield wiper. It is especially effective in defending against a puck carrier attempting a wide wraparound. It's an aggressive move that requires strength and a quick recovery. It should be used only on the stick side.

To perform this technique, drop *one knee* to the ice while sweeping around with the goal stick. Your arm and shoulder should be extended so that the full length of the stick is flat on the ice. The stick may not always reach the puck, but it will at least force the puck carrier wider. Be prepared to quickly recover your ready stance or continue to aggressively pursue the puck in another manner.

When executing this move, the high short side may be a problem. Keep your shoulders square and your trapper open to provide maximum coverage. Always keep your skates ready to push and challenge or in a position that will allow you to quickly recover to your feet.

The sweep check is a relatively simple skill, but as with all save skills, timing is very important. Too early or too obvious a move, for example, will allow the shooter time to change his tactics. So you should talk with your defensemen about how to deal with a wraparound play.

Remember: the sweep check's zone is the space between the post on the stick side and the puck. Yet you still need to keep your head on a swivel to be aware of off-puck players.

Lunge Check

Generally, the lunge check is used to redirect a loose puck far from the net (between the dots and the blue line). Often, it is preceded by a footrace between the goalie and an attacker. It is a breathtaking play for coaches and fans. Trouble can occur for the goalie if he is a slower skater, if he leaves the net wide open, or if he stays prone on the ice after the lunge.

The timing of the lunge is a function of the goalie's attributes: foot speed, decision making, and physical strength. The goalie should be skating hard, holding his stick held at the knob and out front with the blade *on the ice*. The most effective lunges begin about ten feet, or two stick lengths, from the puck. Otherwise, time is lost and the lunge may be for nought.

When you reach for the puck, your stick blade should be angled so that the puck deflects away from the play action. The last thing

If there is a race for the puck in your zone, a lunge check may be employed. A forward and a goalie racing toward the puck in open ice is one of hockey's most exciting plays.

you want is to make a perfect pass to the shooter. Proper clearing allows you time to recover. The lunge check should proceed as follows: race, lunge, poke, recover to your feet, and skate quickly back into position while keeping your eye on the puck.

A special note about all aggressive moves: if you are not sure, don't leave the net. Any hesitation whatsoever means lost time and space, which gives the shooter an edge.

Paddle-Down Saves

The paddle-down skill provides coverage of the low half of the net. The stick's built-up section is placed on the ice along with the blade of the stick, pointed up. This technique is typically executed in conjunction with a half-butterfly leg save.

As with the sweep check, you are committing yourself. Therefore, it is important that your shoulders stay up and your hands stay ahead for better short-side coverage. Should the puck carrier pull away from the net, you will have to pursue the puck (with your stick and/or your

When an opponent tries to come out from behind the net for a wraparound, you can use the paddle-down technique to take away the lower portion of the net.

If the opponent doesn't shoot right away on the wraparound, you will need to use the paddle-down-with-puck-pursuit technique, attacking the puck, sliding across the crease, and following the shooter.

trapper) to again force the shooter away from the net and to maintain good gap control for an eventual shot. Basically, this means you should push off the post and go at the puck carrier.

Puck Control

A more advanced goalie may, instead of setting up the puck for a teammate behind the net, be called on to aggressively move the puck out of the zone himself. This can take one of many forms: (1) You can scoop up the puck with your stick and flip it out of the zone at or beyond center ice. (2) You can devise a set play such as a hard, long pass to a forward positioned on your side of the red line in the referee's crease. Patrick Roy and the Colorado Avalanche use this play often. (3) You can fire a high, hard clearing pass off the glass to get the puck out of your zone. Ed Belfour is one of the best at this trick. (4) You may get a little bold, toss the puck up, and bat it to center ice, as Dominik Hasek does. (5) You might try the Corsi drop kick, where the puck is tossed up and kicked out of the zone soccer-style (then again, maybe not!).

Active goalie input involves both stopping and playing pucks, but before you can play the puck you have to field it. So fielding the puck is another important element of a goalie's toolbox.

Here is a superb example of Dominik Hasek providing active input into the game through puck handling.

This is the hand placement you should have when passing or shooting a puck on your forehand. The top hand is ahead and away from your hip as the lower hand pushes down and through a forward motion.

One benefit of having a goalie who is a good puck handler is that he can be the first phase of his team's offense, much as a soccer goalie will distribute the ball in a variety of ways to start his team's offense. More so than ever before, goalies are fielding loose pucks behind the net and in the corners.

For example, an attacking team will often dump the puck into the offensive zone. When this happens, the goalie can play the puck himself—almost like a third defenseman. This disrupts the opposing team's attack and sets up the goalie's team to quickly clear the defensive zone. Stopping the puck behind the net, moving it to a defenseman, clearing it—all of these moves help a team's offense immensely.

Two-Handed Puck Handling

When shooting or passing, always keep your hands (or gloves) clear of your body. The blocker as the top hand should be ahead and away from your hips. Push down into the ice with your lower hand (the

Here is the way you can move the puck on your backhand using a one-handed slap. Notice how your knees should be bent to generate more power.

trapper hand). This also prevents the stick from flying over the puck and missing it. Passing, or wristing, requires rolling the puck from the heel to the toe of the blade. It is generally best to sweep the puck where the pass is to go, using the bottom hand. The top hand's wrist should roll as if it were executing a wrist shot. At the same instant, the top hand, which is ahead of your body, is snapped backward. For backhand flipping, use the middle or heel of the goalie stick blade. Blades that have too big a curve inhibit this move, which is another reason to have a straight blade or one with a shallow curve.

Reverse Two-Handed Puck Handling

A left-handed-catching goalie with a natural right-handed shot (or vice versa) has a stick-handling challenge. Of course, this situation may actually result in easier and better stick handling. But there are usually disadvantages: time is lost switching the stick over from one side to the other, long clearings are more difficult, and the blade is curved in the wrong direction.

Practice switching the stick over by rolling your stick (like a baton) so that the stick's knob is caught by the trapper. Jam the butt end of the stick into the palm of the trapper (the top hand) and squeeze. Forehand clearing may not be strong, but backhanded passes will probably be exceptional.

One-Handed Puck Handling

One-handed forehand and backhand passes are necessary for quick-up clearings and passes. If a goalie is strong enough, his blocker hand, holding the stick alone and slapping or sweeping the puck, usually can move the puck efficiently. Often, the top of the stick shaft can be placed against the goalie's blocker-side hip for leverage. A quick snap down at the puck, using the hip as a pivot, is a good way to backhand the puck one-handed. On the forehand, one-handed pushes are generally effective for short clears or passes.

Puck-Handling Decisions

Stick-handling techniques, as you can see, vary depending on your talent, strength, and the situation. It will all come together over time

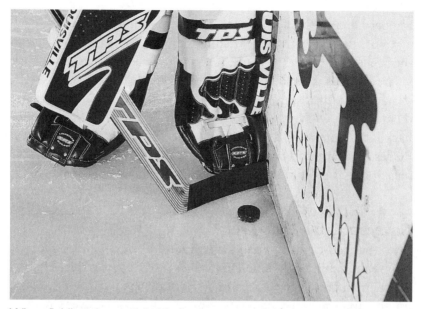

When fielding the puck behind your net on the trapper side, put the blade of your stick against the boards, angle your stick slightly toward the boards, and use your pad as a backup.

When fielding the puck behind your net on the blocker side, place your stick behind you and push the toe of your stick against the boards, and angle your stick blade slightly toward the boards.

To field the puck behind your net on the blocker side, use the skate-blade combo with your stick: push the toe of your skate against the boards, angle your skate blade to the boards slightly, and bring your stick blade toward that skate's heel as a backup.

with good practice. The goalie's decision on what to do with the puck is at least as important as proper execution. Pass? Leave? Clear? Freeze? What you do depends on your read of the play.

When it comes to stick handling, active input means direct involvement in your team's next action. First, you must understand that when you stray from the net to field the puck, you leave the net wide open. The decision to field the puck and pass requires good timing, skating skill, quickness, and a good grasp of the play that is developing. Communication between a goalie and his teammates is vitally important. The goalie should understand his team's set plays, paying close attention during chalk talks and strategy discussions.

If you decide to leave a puck rather than pass it, it is always best to leave it at the side of the net and slightly behind the goal line— never in front. The puck should be two to three feet (one meter) from the post, close enough to reach and cover it or poke it away.

Fielding Behind the Net

If you go behind the net to stop and place a puck, it should be left at least six inches (15 cm) from the boards. To stop the puck on a dump-in along the boards, always try to angle your stick, skate, or body toward the boards. This avoids deflecting the puck toward the front of the net.

The discussion that follows describes techniques for stopping the puck behind the net. In our examples, the goalie has a left-handed trapper and a left-handed shot.

Trapper Side. Butt the left leg pad's outside edge against the boards with your left skate blade parallel to the boards. Slightly angle the stick toward the boards and push the toe of the stick into the boards in front of your skate blade. Stop the puck and place it away from the boards.

Blocker Side. Lead with the toe of your stick blade and push it into the boards at a slight angle. The stick should be behind you. Keep your right skate parallel, not perpendicular, to the boards. Again, place the puck away from the boards.

Lead with the right skate, pointing it as you would for a T-glide. Put your right toe into the boards at an angle. Keep your blocker ahead of you and try to keep as much of the stick blade on the ice as possible.

In all situations, don't permit a teammate to skate between you and the net, don't hide the puck, and quickly return to your net. Also, talk with your teammates to avoid miscues with them. Your ears can serve as teammates' eyes! Speak up! Be your teammates' eyes! Communication helps the goalie. Make the right decisions.

10 Communication Opportunities

Off-puck threat: "Watch number 12!"

Off-puck threat: "Watch the trailer!"

Forechecker coming hard: "On you, on you!"

Icing: "Icing!" or "No icing!"

Relieve pressure: "Freeze it!" or "Ice it!"

Rebound loose: "It's loose!" or "It's in your feet!"

Face-off positioning error: "Wait!"

Screen situation: "Screen!"

Situations: "10 seconds!" or "Even strength!" or "Man down!"

Scoring threat: "Hanger!" or "Floater!" or "Man in front!"

7

Game and Player Awareness

Save skills are the necessary reactions to a shot. Learning to play and react as a goalie require a specific strategy: how and when to apply a save skill. Net awareness, angles, telescoping, and gap control are important technical skills that enhance or strengthen the save skill.

A constant message throughout this book has been that *save skills* will define *how* the goalie makes the save, but his *on-ice position* will determine *if* he makes the save. The goalie must be between the net and the shot—in the shot lane. Remember our simple checklist: "Where's the puck, where's the post, where am I?"

On-ice goalie position is influenced by many factors. Where is the action coming from? Where is it going? What type of play is developing? Who's the defenseman? Who's the shooter? When the action quickly changes, the goalie has to follow (track) the play—know the players' positions and try to imagine where they will go. Tracking the play must be done compactly and quickly as the play action changes. Being in the correct on-ice position requires (1) being in the line of fire between the puck and the net—in the shot lane, and (2) challenging with good gap control between you and the shooter.

Net awareness is key to on-ice positioning and angles. Here's an interesting way to think about it: you, as the goalie for your team, must track the game as if you are bringing the net along with you. In this way, you use the net to your advantage. By always knowing where the net is, you can get to the exact position you need to be in with no time lost searching for the net. If you achieve good gap control, the angles will work to your advantage, not the shooter's.

Along with good skating skills, tracking the play properly is key to a goalie's success. "Where's the puck? Where's the post? Where do I want to be?": these are three important questions during play action to which a goalie must have immediate answers. Net awareness is knowing where you are in relation to the net and the play.

Really having it takes a lot of practice at being in control and in position. The goalie who controls his own position well always knows where the net is.

Tracking

Always keep your head on a "swivel." This is a fundamental rule for all players in the defensive zone—including goalies. Knowing where off-puck players are (those who do not possess the puck) provides cues for the goalie to anticipate where the puck will go and from which area of the ice the action might come. Then there's no need to "look and go." You can just go! Thinking less and doing less makes you faster. Keep your eye on the puck and continuously check for the other players (your teammates, too). This is tracking the play. Think of it as following the big picture of the game. In all situations, goalies should use this strategy to improve their game. An important rule for goalies is this: "Focus on the puck, see the play."

Peripheral Vision

Peripheral vision is both a natural and a learned skill. With his eyes focused on the puck, a goalie's peripheral vision allows him to see and notice players and activity off the puck. You can practice this skill both on and off the ice. For example, sitting in your room, try focusing on a puck and seeing the other objects in the room without really taking your eyes off the puck.

Low to High Tracking (From the Corner)

When the puck carrier starts in the corner and then carries the puck up the boards (low to high), the goaltender's positioning should change as the puck moves toward the blue line. Basically, as the puck is carried away from the corner and toward the hash marks along the boards to the top of the circle, the goalie should track the play from the *short* side. When a shot occurs, the goalie's motion should be toward the middle of the shot lane.

"Shuffle" skating (see Chapter 5) is key to good tracking. While you are shuffling, your ready stance should track square to the puck, your shoulders, hands, and stick (in front of skates) facing the puck. Like a wall, and staying compact, you move off the near post to maximize net coverage as you track from low to high.

Behind-the-Net Tracking (Paddle Down)

When a puck carrier is behind the net, the goalie tracks while anticipating a wraparound or quick centering pass. Here, the active position of the goal stick is aggressive. The goalie's stance on the post is the same as if the puck were in the corner. The stick is actively placed in the passing lane just off the post. Tracking from post to post, the stick tracks the puck movement. The overall technique revolves around three basic keys:

- Don't leave the puck-side post. Keep your shoulders and hands ahead and only rotate your head, looking through the net to view the puck. If the player crosses the middle of the net, go to the other post. Basically, be on one post or the other at all times. Don't get caught in no-man's-land.
- When you do move to the other post, go quickly and lead with your stick blade to the inside of the other post as you push (your stick will get there faster). Should a wraparound be attempted, drive your blocker into the ice. This will bring your paddle down to meet the puck.
- The skating push is either a T-push (youths) or a shuffle (older and stronger players). Use whichever is faster for you. As your skate arrives at the post, simultaneously reassume your ready stance. Always try to have the inside edge of one skate biting into the ice. This will enable you to burst out quickly should a quick centering pass occur.

115

Effective use of the paddle-down during a wraparound is a valuable skill. Remember to pursue the puck should the puck carrier come out in front of the net. Be aggressive and attack the puck, paddle down, keeping your shoulders up and your trapper ahead and your leg extended (like a straight-leg half butterfly) as the puck carrier moves off post and through the crease. This attacking paddle down will force the puck carrier into traffic in front of the net and take the angle away with good gap control (see "Paddle-Down Saves" and accompanying photos in Chapter 6).

Angles

Once you leave the net, you should know exactly where the net is in relation to the puck and yourself. If you are in the shot lane with a compact stance and, ideally, at the top of the crease or closer to the puck carrier (gap control), you are providing good net coverage. You may not even have to make an actual save. Sometimes the best saves occur when the puck just hits the goalie or misses the net entirely.

Coming out to cut down the angle usually results in square challenges with good gap control. But what if there is a wide pass? Sometimes it is a long trip from one side of the crease to the other. In this case, coming out too far ultimately results in poor net coverage (i.e., poor net gap control).

In effect, playing angles makes the net smaller. Squared-up on-ice positioning cuts shooting angles and shrinks targets. When goalies actively challenge, this puts the shooter under pressure: Where do I shoot now? Do I pass? Do I deke? The puck carrier's hesitation gives the goalie and his team time and space to recover and defend.

The angles we're talking about are those formed by three points: the near post, the puck, and the far post (see Figure 7.1). The goalie must be positioned inside the triangle formed by those three points—ideally, centered directly in the shot lane. Gaining this on-ice posi-

Figure 7.1

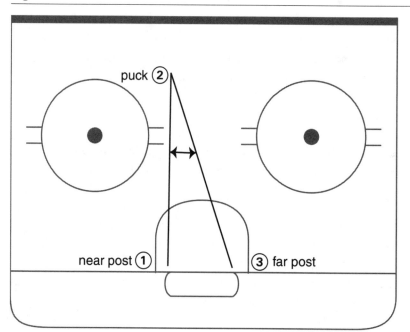

tion repeatedly takes a lot of practice and solid skating skills. Remember: quick and compact movements save time for the goalie. This is an example of that principle at work.

10 of the Most Common Mistakes That Lead to Goals

Too deep in the net (gap control)
Inability to control rebounds
Committing too early
Poor angle play
Mishandling the puck
Double coverage in stance (off-balance ready stance)
Legs too far apart or too close, locking knees
Failure to communicate or focus
Stick not on the ice
Being surprised by a shot or play

Of course, the angle enlarges and shrinks as the play moves: The closer the puck is to the boards, the smaller the angle at the top of the triangle; the closer the puck is to the net, the bigger the angle.

As the angle increases, the net becomes more open. However, if you come out too far to shrink (or cut) the angle, you will have to go farther to pursue lateral puck movements. This is an excellent example of a goalie doing too much. It's a case of diminishing returns. The better your gap with the net, the shorter the distance you have to cover laterally. Suddenly, you become even faster. As a rule, top-of-the-crease positioning is good angle play (at least as a starting point).

117

Telescoping

Telescoping is moving forward and backward in the shot lane to maintain good angles and good gap control. Sometimes the goalie needs a reference point as he moves out of the net. Use your stick or glove to bang a post; in other words, bring a piece of the net with you. Then move out into the shot lane and get into position. Try to do all this without turning your head to look at the net; rely on your peripheral vision

When returning, or backing in, to the net, young goalies often stare at the post. Avoid this! Glance rapidly once at the near post, which gives you the line of return. A goalie must have confidence and visualize the net in his mind. Sometimes, when the play is developing slowly, it's OK to glance more than once—but never get caught staring at the post. Make sure that your glance is at the *near post only* (or short-side post). Otherwise, you will have a tendency to rotate your shoulders back and forth, which will cause you to zigzag and go off line. At the youth level, short-side goals are often the result of this mistake. As a rule, look over your left shoulder for the left post during attacks from the right wing and over your right shoulder for the right post during attacks from the left wing.

A word for coaches: Gap control usually refers to that important space between the onrushing forward and the retreating defenseman. For goaltenders, gap control is the only way to cut down angles.

Coming too far out from the net allows the attacking players to initiate a lateral attack, putting time on the opponent's side. Getting out late gives the puck carrier a lot of net to shoot at—and enough time to reach the net. A blast or deke usually follows, and frequently the result is a goal.

Getting back to the net too slowly may also create problems. An attacker can simply skate by the goalie, deke laterally, and get to the net much more quickly than a slowly backward-moving goalie can.

The telescope technique requires sudden and abrupt stops and starts. Time spent slowing to a stop or bursting forward is time given to the attackers. At the other extreme, a rushed charge also works in favor of the shooter.

"A skating goalie is often a beaten goalie" is one of our adages. If the goalie's feet are busy skating forward, save skills are difficult to execute. If there is a lateral pass, or a quick shot, or a rebound, the goalie is frequently caught off balance. Telescoping is not only about sudden, abrupt starts and stops. It is timed movement that takes away time and net from the shooter, gives the goaltender time and space to return to the net, or allows him to move laterally into the shot lane to track a lateral play-action. But telescoping is effective only if the goalie's skating and decision-making abilities are sound. So speed, skating skills, and timing are the essentials of telescoping. "When" (timing) and "where" (position) are the essence of gap control, the *result of telescoping.*

Gap Control

As mentioned earlier, gap control conventionally refers to that space between the shooter and the defenseman. In today's goaltending, there are two points of reference: the distance between the goalie and shooter, and the distance between the goalie and net (see Figure 7.2). Gap control directly affects net coverage and the goalie's ability to track play action efficiently. A goalie should challenge the play with consistent net coverage and by filling in the shot lane with maximum net coverage during an at-net rush or lateral play-action.

From any point on the ice, only so much of the four-by-six-foot net is open to the shooter. Telescoping and gap control cut down the angles from which an offensive player can shoot and thus can give an advantage to the goaltender. To be a useful strategy in a game situation, telescoping must be a controlled technique that uses gap control to reduce a shooter's target.

The following facts are important when considering gap control, angles, and net coverage:

- The farther the goalie is out toward the puck, the less net is available to shoot at.
- Coverage is not improved much by being too far out and overplaying the shooter—a pass play can be a problem.
- The farther the puck is from the net, the smaller the angle.
- The closer the puck is to the boards, the smaller the angle.

Figure 7.2

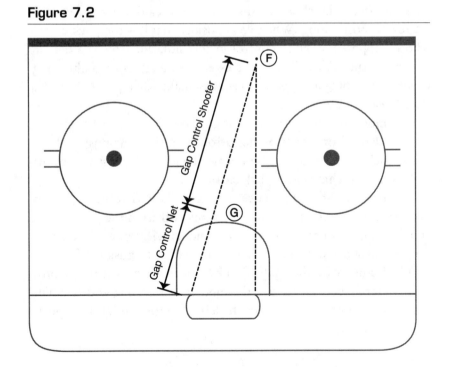

Essentially, a point of diminishing returns is reached if you venture too far out from the net. But if you are not out far enough, the puck is just as likely to blast by you. Effective gap control reduces these risks (see Figures 7.3 and 7.4).

When a goalie comes out to challenge the shooter, he must be aware of the shooter's speed. The goalie achieves good gap control between himself and the shooter when he shows as little of the net as possible while remaining close enough to recover or move to the shot lane if the play moves laterally.

Gap-Control Techniques. As the shooter approaches, appropriate gap control (shooter-goalie and goalie-net) as the goalie backs in provides consistent net coverage. Of course, most attackers can skate forward faster than a goalie can skate backward; yet proper gap control by the goalie will show minimal net to the approaching shooter. Cutting angles is the result of using telescoping and gap control, denying time and space to the shooter. That puts pressure on the shooter and gives the advantage to the goalie and the defense.

Aggressive positioning puts pressure on the shooter by showing a smaller net. Pressure increases on the shooter as the shooter gets closer—less and less net is shown. During a net drive or rush, the puck carrier may find he has little net to shoot at and be forced to pass. In effect, the shooter falls into a trap caused by the goalie's aggressive positioning. When you consider that it is the puck carrier who is supposed to be in control in this situation, this is a definite turning of the tables. That is the essence of aggressive goaltending. Proper telescoping and good gap control make you a proactive rather than a reactive goaltender.

It is important to remember that gap control and good angle play directly depend on net awareness. Touching the near post with the goalie stick or the trapper as you leave the net is the best way to orient yourself to challenge a puck carrier.

Young goalies should practice skating skills so that their telescoping is true and straight. Often goalies push off from the post off-line and then adjust for the shooter. This is not efficient or effective, since it results in short-side openings. One remedy is to push off from the post by leading with the goalie's stick blade to the proper on-ice position. Maintain being square to the shooter by stopping with the right skate (off the right near post) or the left skate (off the left near post).

Figure 7.3

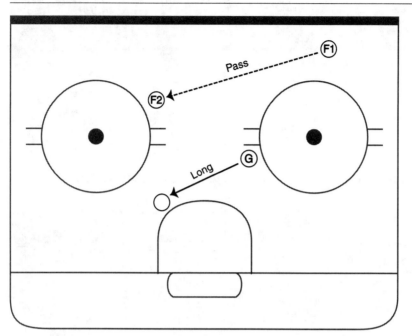

Figure 7.4

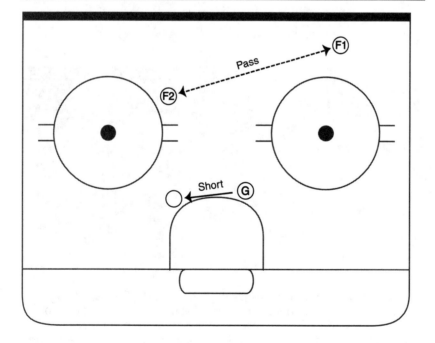

Gap control: You must come out to challenge the shooter.

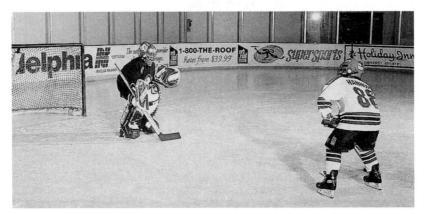

As the shooter advances, you slowly retreat.

Remember, you must maintain two gaps properly: One is the gap between you and the shooter in front of you. The other is the gap between you and the net behind you. Maximize your net coverage with good gap control, as shown here. Note that the goalie is at the edge of his crease when the shot occurs.

Another flaw is bobbing up and down as you skate, which can cause the stick to lift off the ice. When skating, you should maintain a constant ready stance: the legs and upper body should move independently of each other. When skating forward or backward, push your stick into the ice. Practice net-awareness drills and try to keep your eyes on a fixed point at the top of the boards. If no bobbing occurs, the board's top will appear to stay level.

Skating backward, the goalie must focus on the shooter and maintain good gap control. Remember, as a goalie gets better, usually a glance at the short-side post is enough to assure him he has good position. In general, young goalies should work on net awareness and controlling their movements within about a stick length's radius around the net. One excellent way to perfect this is to practice the W, X, Y, and Z net-awareness drills outlined in Chapter 10 (the pros do these all the time).

Awareness of Player Positioning

At higher levels of play (age 15 and older), another factor comes into play. Awareness, at this level, refers not only to net awareness, but also to awareness of player positioning.

In today's game, the goalie and the defense should work together. This means that a team's defensive system has one more active member: the goalie. As your team's goalie, you must know the whereabouts and intentions of the opposing team's shooters—including their obvious (slot) and less obvious (back-door) options. In addition, you have to know where your own teammates are. By knowing your opponents' positions and their movements, you will have the clues necessary to anticipate developing plays. Recall that "head on a swivel" means moving your head to check on other players off the puck (your teammates as well)—yet never losing track of the player with the puck! Remember our saying: *Focus on the puck and see the play.*

When you know how your defense will react to game situations and vice versa, you've achieved an integrated defensive system. To bring it all together, timing, positioning, and systems (for all defenders) are needed. It takes practice, communication, and patience to execute a total team defensive strategy.

8

Game Situations

Your style as a goalie should be all your own. Techniques and skills vary, but, as we have seen, there are basic tools that are common to all styles. How a goalie uses these tools during game situations will define his success within his style. Remember that style determines *how* the goalie makes a save; positioning determines *if* he makes the save. During a game, the goalie must maintain focus on the play. Ideal concentration is the shutting out of distractions, but not to the point where you can't react effectively to the play going on around you. On the ice, you cannot be distracted by parents, noisy fans, goal-mouth traffic, or vocal opponents. You must find a way to block out these nuisances and maintain focus on the job at hand: to work the game and play the best hockey you can.

The ability to react properly during play action is influenced by many factors. A goalie's skill techniques are being put to effective use when he tracks the play, stays square, and gains the shot lane—all in an effort to maximize net coverage. We see it as being a goalie on the S.P.O.T.: Square, Prepared, and on Time.

Tracking Play Action

Goaltenders are part of team play. Stopping the puck is their number-one job, but it is actually the end result of many actions. Use of save skills, fielding pucks, and so on, are all part of a goalie's job during a game. To be effective, a goalie must be able to track the play.

Tracking simply means following the play, much as a fighter pilot watches a formation of enemy jets. It is essential to know where the player with the puck is at all times, to focus on the puck, and to see the play develop. Equally important, you must know which of the opposition players without the puck pose a threat. At the same time, you have to stay in the shot lane and maintain consistent gap control

KID'S KEY: SHOWING CHARACTER

- Be the hardest-working player on your team.
- Pay attention and learn the whole game of hockey.
- Work for the team and the team will work for you!

in relation to both the net and the shooter. To visualize this in your own mind, think of yourself as being at the narrow end of a funnel. To stop as many shots as possible, you want to be in position to plug the end of the funnel.

10 Ways to Stay Alert During a Game

Up/Downs
Side-to-Side Skating
W, X, Y, and Z Skating Drills (see Chapter 10)
Post touches
Drinking of fluids
Simulated catches
Dividing the game into segments
Review opponents
Visualization
Squawking

Tracking is done with your eyes and your feet, so skating skills and compact movement are vitally important to tracking. Goalies must continually work on these skills. Having your head "on a swivel" (an old motto for defensemen) gives you a view of the whole game. Moving your feet keeps you consistently in the shot lane. Here's the way we like to think of it: goalies play hockey *and* they stop pucks!

It's important that your knees are always bent, especially when you stop or start. Bent knees give more balance and agility. They also allow you to be ready to spring into action. Ready mind, ready stance, and compact body—these are the traits of an alert, reactive goalie. Quick, reactive thrusts and sharp, quick stops also save valuable time when you are under attack by opposing skaters. Mastering these techniques will make you a much quicker goalie.

127

Going to the Shot Lane

To be a successful goaltender, you have to know where to position yourself—and when.

Imagine a direct line drawn from point A (the puck) to point B (the middle of the net). That line is called the shot lane. While tracking the play, a goalie must be standing on that line and have good gap control with the shooter. To have any chance of stopping a shot, the goalie has to be in the shot lane when the shot occurs. In other words, you must position yourself directly in the line of fire!

Often, young goalies question coaches about which particular tool or piece of equipment to use when making a save. That is understandable, but a goalie should first be told that getting to the shot

KID'S KEY: PLAYING GOALIE

- Always be looking to add techniques to your toolbox.
- Be active and influence the flow of the game.
- Get to the shot lane first.

128

lane is a much more important concern—and that fast feet and good skating skills will allow a goalie to get to the shot lane more quickly.

During side-to-side play, you must be extremely observant. For example, if the puck is passed, you must be able to anticipate where the shot will come from before making your move to the shot lane. Going to the shot lane square, prepared, and on time ("S.P.O.T.") gives you a chance to make the save with maximum net coverage.

Once you are in position to challenge the shot, you can read, predict, interpret, and react with a save skill. Regardless of the level of competition, during a game your skills and abilities will turn instinctive at this point—that is, you will have very little time to think.

Step-By-Step Play-Action Strategy

Tracking the play, seeing it develop, reading the possibilities, and reacting to the play are all part of goaltending at its highest level—but acquiring these abilities takes practice and experience. The model goaltender in the game today—the one player who does all these things more consistently than anyone else—is Dominik Hasek. He has an uncanny ability to think like a forward and play like a goalie.

The following steps analyze the play-action strategy for saves:

1. Track the Play: focus on the puck while absorbing the bigger picture.
   - Keep ready stance compact
   - Move laterally
   - Maintain proper gap with shooter
   - Maintain proper gap with net
   - Maximize net coverage
   - Lots of communication

2. Read the Possibilities: determine the numerous possible threats that are developing in real time.
   - "Head on swivel"
   - Darting eyes (peripheral vision)
   - Net awareness
   - Off-puck player positions
3. Predict the Attack: anticipate what is most likely to happen next.
   - Think like the shooter
   - Know players' whereabouts (yours and theirs), coverage, and next-nearest danger
   - Recognize limitations (strengths and weaknesses of players in situation)
4. React Using a Tool: decide which one of the many save skills in your goalie's toolbox you will use, and act.
   - Passive, aggressive, or combination approach
   - Square to puck
   - Quickness and reflexes
   - Go with instinct—don't hesitate

5. Recover and Reset: reposition yourself after having made the first save.
- Continue puck pursuit (in shot lane or at puck)
- Have fast feet (use of skates); get edges into the ice
- Return to ready stance
- Track play action (begin again!)

From defending against an odd-man rush to penalty killing, a goalie must be aware of his team's defensive tactics. Team tactics vary with the level of competition and coaching styles, but in all cases, the goalie works game situations with the single objective of stopping the puck. The strategy outlined above applies at all levels. Goalies' strength, age, and ability vary, but all goaltenders should work toward meeting these objectives.

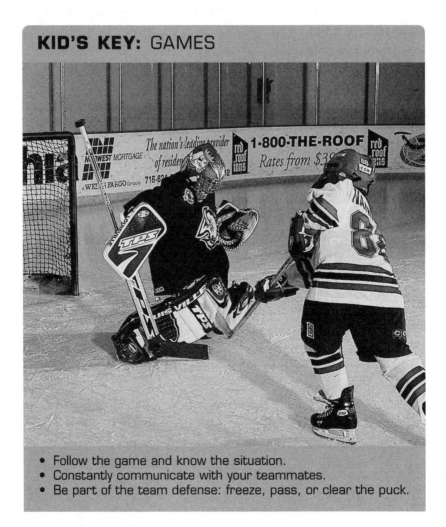

KID'S KEY: GAMES

- Follow the game and know the situation.
- Constantly communicate with your teammates.
- Be part of the team defense: freeze, pass, or clear the puck.

Staying Square in the Shot Lane

"Staying square" is an advanced technique that a goalie uses while moving laterally. The goalie's position relative to the shooter and relative to the net is a straight line. Net coverage is especially affected by a goalie's lateral movements, so a goalie may be forced to assume a sideways stance when defending against a player or puck moving laterally.

This is a great example of how being square provides you with maximum net coverage.

To maintain proper net coverage as the play gradually moves from side to side, short lateral shuffles (creating almost a circular movement) are ideal. Of course, when the play is sudden and quick, a straight line is the best and shortest route. Get to the shot lane!

Good skating skills will allow you to stay square or square up during play action. Younger goalies may prefer T-glides for tracking, but they should work toward acquiring a strong shuffle for lateral skating. Squaring up is done by using the "triangle of hands and stick blade" tracking technique: Bring the triangle squarely into the shot lane. Your shoulders and feet will adjust as you square up.

Playing Goalie

To develop the tools for game situations, a strong skill base is needed. Individual and team concepts have common characteristics that are important to goalies' development at all levels. Now we will expand upon some of the general themes mentioned above.

Focus on the Game

Follow the action at both ends and try to influence the flow of the game. For example, a timely freeze of the play action can give your team a much-needed chance to change lines. Your focus should be your play not only as a goalie but as a player on the team. So be in the game and follow it as it develops. Know where offensive and defensive players are on the ice. Feel the tempo of the game.

Communicate

Talk with your coaching staff and teammates before, during, and after games. This way, everyone will be working the game in the same manner. During the game, the goalie has an excellent view of the game. By talking to his defensemen, he can help the defense to read situations. For defensemen, "let your ears be your eyes" is a communication key. Defenders who can hear their goalie gain knowledge about the situation on the ice without losing concentration on their puck pursuit. Communication keeps the team working well together, and this limits the opponents' goal-scoring chances.

Keep Your Feet

If you must go down onto the ice, it should be to get the puck, to maximize net coverage, or to make a save. Once you drop down, you have committed yourself and, therefore, must get a skate edge into the ice. Otherwise, a lateral play or any other change in the play may result in a "drop and reach" reaction—that is, when a downed goalie must lunge or reach without any traction from his skates. Staying square and tracking in the shot lane make you play "bigger." Your feet get you where you need to be and are the keys to effective puck pursuit and tracking.

Active Input

In today's game, the age-old rule of not making the first move still holds, but today's goalie must provide active input—that is, be more aggressive. This is a theme we have preached throughout this book. For example, active input may come in the form of a quick poke check. However, there is a fine line between an aggressive move and committing too early (i.e., making the first move). Make sure that the attacker has fallen into your defensive trap; then a first move can be effective. You don't necessarily have to make the first move—just be in position to react first. And remember: there is nothing wrong with an aggressive mistake, as long as you learn from it.

Gap Control

Gap control refers to the goalie's gap with the shooter and with the net. If you have good shooter gap, the attacker sees little net; if you have good net gap, you are close enough to the net to stymie lateral (side-to-side) plays. Your level of play, backward-skating ability, and lateral-skating ability all affect the gap. Good gap control requires good telescoping.

Work with Your Feet

Agility, balance, and skating speed are all part of good goaltending. Frequent off-ice training can enhance your footwork, resulting in light, quick feet. Remember: your feet and legs should work independently of your hands, head, and shoulders during on-ice movement!

Imaging/Visualizing

When called upon to react during a game, you will have little time to think. So it is useful to simulate game situations in your mind beforehand. Put yourself into the play; positively reinforce the fact that you are in the play and *making the save*. See yourself succeed. Go over reading and reacting to plays, imaging the proper reaction by you, the goalie. Imaging allows your body to react properly without having to think first. You've seen this situation before, and your mind knows how your body should react.

10 Ways to Relieve Pressure During Play

Freeze the puck
Ice the puck
Displace the net (*Caution*: you may be risking a penalty.)
Take a penalty
Shout encouragement to teammates
Adjust equipment (pads/gloves)
Shoot puck over the boards (*Caution*: you may be risking a penalty.)
Set up slowly during stoppages
Talk to the referee
Ask to change your stick at the bench

Playing Breakaways

One of the most exciting plays in hockey is the breakaway—for everyone other than the shooter and the goalie, that is. Breakaways usually bring fans out of their seats, and they almost always change the momentum of the game.

Breakaways can take many forms—up the middle, down the wing, or even a penalty shot. In addition, the pursuit of an attacker can range from none (penalty shot) to strong (your teammate within a stick's length of the attacker).

There are several things you can do to minimize the chance you'll be scored on during a breakaway. First, you need to be following the game at all times so you are not surprised when a breakaway occurs. Second, you can try to make the shooter miss. Come out past the top of the crease and retreat backward slowly. Focus on the puck, not his body or eyes. Let him commit first, then react accordingly. Third, for shots other than penalty shots, it is not enough to just make the initial save—you've got to control the rebound, too. Finally, if you are scored upon (this occurs only 20 to 30 percent of the time), don't rant and rave. Doing so will only give your opponents a psychological advantage. Here are some types of breakaways and other situations a goalie encounters:

One-Man Breakaway (1:0)

When facing a breakaway, be in the challenging position before the shooter is ready to make a move. As for your on-ice position, often two or three feet (one meter) in front of the crease is good. Remember: most breakaway shot attempts are thwarted. The law of averages is on your side—act like it!

Begin backing in after the attacker has entered the slot area between the circles. Gap control is important. A good drill to simulate this situation is the Y Drill (see Chapter 10) with "1-2 Backward" thrust toward the net. One visual cue for you is the forward's stick. If he is handling the puck at his side, it usually means a shot. If his

One-man breakaway: In this situation it helps to know the shooter's tendencies (but this may not always be possible). More important, maintain good gap control to deny net area. Work on your Y Drill to improve your timing. If you keep a balanced ready stance, you will be better prepared to react to a deke.

stick is out in front, it usually means a deke. However, good scorers mask their intentions.

Good net coverage (gap with shooter) can force the shooter to change his plans. Likewise, a good, quick poke check can surprise the forward if he shows any hesitation (very common in youth hockey). Remember, try to refrain from lunging during a poke check. Maintain your backward skating to the net. Estimate how much help you will get from your teammates after the save and how long it will take for them to get there.

One-on-One (1:1)

Always play the puck carrier as if he is going to shoot. Be in position, expecting a quick release through or along the side of your defenseman's skates.

The defenseman should know not to back in too far and to keep the puck carrier away from the critical shooting zone (the slot). The defenseman does this by angling the puck carrier away from the slot and toward the boards, not back in onto his goalie.

Should the puck carrier get around the defenseman, the goalie must track this move, stay in the shot lane, and maintain good gap con-

One-on-one: Nothing against your defenseman, but you have to expect that the worst will happen here—he may get beat. So anticipate the shooter's options by staying square with a good gap (shooter and net). Odds are the shooter will try to force a shot through your defenseman's legs.

trol. Sometimes the puck carrier will try to cut across the front of the net. A good sweep or poke check (with a ready lateral move by the goalie) can dislodge the puck or trip up the attacker. A good butterfly with lateral motion to pursue the puck can also be effective. In effect, one-on-one is really one attacker on two defenders when the goalie and defense work together. A good drill for one-on-one tracking is the Z Drill (see Chapter 10).

Two-Man Breakaway (2:0)

At the youth level, two-man breaks occur more often than coaches and goalies would like. The key to defending a two-on-none is to try to force your opponents into making a bad or unnecessary pass or get them to take a low-percentage (backhand, bad angle, hurried) shot. Size up the situation, determine how you want the play to flow, and try to influence the outcome. Focus on the puck, look for cues as to whether the opponent will pass or shoot, and know where the off-puck player is. No one is going to blame you for giving up a goal on a two-on-none. Good gap control with the net allows for you to react to a pass. Avoid overplaying or over-challenging the shooter—the edge of the crease is good positioning here. The X Drill (see Chapter 10) is a good tracking exercise for two-on-none situations.

Two-man breakaway: This doesn't happen much in the pros, but it sure does in youth hockey. Knowing your opponents will help. Who is the goal scorer? Who is the setup man? Is either player on his off wing? Where is the backchecker coming from? Your best approach is to be at the edge of the crease when a shot or pass occurs (good gap control). Here you'll be in the best position to stop the shot or react to a pass.

Two-on-One (2:1)

The two-on-one is a common and very dangerous odd-man situation. The goalie must be included as part of team defensive tactics in this case. The goalie should always play the shooter, trying to read signs that a pass or shot is coming. The attacking team usually sends the player off the puck hard to the net. However, if the goalie employs active input, it balances the situation to a two-on-two.

With good gap control (start about one foot ahead of the crease), the goalie plays the shot. The defenseman takes out the passing lane. The timing between the defenseman and the goalie is critical. As the puck carrier approaches, his options become fewer if you have good gap control. If you force the puck carrier to hesitate, this closes the gap. Now the combined defense of the goalie and defenseman has taken time and space from the offensive players. The defenseman can then slide backward (feet first) to snuff out the pass.

If a pass play goes to the at-net player, use your half-butterfly, butterfly, or two-pad stack save skills. Go to the shot lane!

If the defenseman can steer the puck carrier to the boards, a poor-angle shot or poor passing situation may result—a more favorable event than two forwards busting up the gut. The goalie is now ready to make a save on the short side, and he can anticipate the centering pass or even deflect the puck. Be careful not to make your first move

Two-on-one: This situation is a common occurrence in games, so you must be a master at defending against it. Quite simply, your job is to take the puck carrier (shooter), and the defenseman's job is to take away the pass. Be sure to communicate about this with your defenseman. Good gap control will intimidate the puck carrier. If he makes a pass and it does get through, go to the shot lane.

too early. Timing is critical! A good practice drill for two-on-one tracking and puck pursuit is the X Drill (see Chapter 10).

Two-on-Two (2:2)

The goalie should know where all the players are in his defensive zone. This is a key for anticipation and very important when traffic increases in your offensive zone.

Like the two-on-one, your initial position should be about one foot in front of the crease. Good gap control is important in reacting to a quick shot, pass, or tip-in. In most situations, the off-puck player charging the net is looking for that tip-in pass or rebound. Focus on the shooter, but anticipate the off-puck player's route. Remember to "focus on the puck and see the play." On the tip-in pass play, use butterfly, half-butterfly, or even two-pad stack save skills. Go to the shot lane with maximum net coverage on the tip-in; pursue the puck.

Keep good position and good gap control, and remain on your skates for tracking and puck pursuit during play action. This allows you and your defensemen to gain time and space, reducing your opponents' easy access to the net. Always remember that the numbers can change if one of your players gets beat or falls and suddenly you are faced with a two-on-one or, worse, a breakaway. Be ready

139

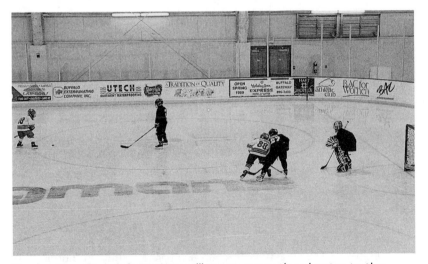

Two-on-two: One defenseman will try to move the shooter to the outside while the other ties up the opponent without the puck. You should always focus on the puck carrier and simultaneously track the off-puck opponent. Dangerous situations you will need to be ready for include a surprise shot through your defenseman and a successful pass to the man without the puck.

and maintain good gap control and tracking in the shot lane. The X and Z Drills (see Chapter 10) are good play-action tracking and gap-control exercises for two-on-two situations.

Three-on-Two (3:2)

As in all odd-man situations, the goaltender's active input plays an important role here. Playing the three-on-two by denying the attackers time and space is an important tactic. The objective is to have one of your backcheckers regain defensive numbers by taking advantage of any offensive delay. The goalie's primary responsibility is to play the puck carrier. By challenging the puck carrier (with good net and shooter gap control), the puck carrier may hesitate—and this works in the defense's favor. However, don't overplay the shooter, which could lead to a difficult recovery if a lateral play-action develops.

When defending against a three-on-two, the goalie must be acutely aware of the players off the puck. He should look for cues as the play develops—especially by reading how attackers off the puck position themselves.

Expect the attackers to overload on one defenseman—isolating him for a two-on-one—while the third attacker drives to the net, taking the other defenseman along with him.

Three-on-two: Here your defensemen are trying to buy time until your team gets another man back to help out. Throughout the attack, the person you need to focus on most is the player with the puck. This is where any scoring chance will start. At the same time, you will need to see the whole ice and anticipate what other scenarios are most likely to occur (drop pass, cross-ice pass, drive to the net, etc.). Focus on the puck and see the play.

Defensemen each have their own responsibilities in three-on-two situations; they are also in a read-and-react situation. However, a goalie with good on-ice position can take away or limit the shot option of the initial puck carrier. This works in favor of the defense—the pass is probably on! And the probability of completing a pass is never 100 percent. With good gap control, passing lanes are restricted and little net is shown. The goalie must be aware of the options available to the puck carrier—having your head "on a swivel" will help you see the play and anticipate play-action changes.

Set plays that the attackers may try include the following: pass, pass for a tip-in, shoot, or deke. The goalie must keep his feet ready to react to the play. Good gap control with the net helps to defend against the lateral pass. Good gap control with the shooter puts pressure on him and maximizes net coverage.

Practice and communication with your defensemen eventually will coordinate your total team defense. The X and Z Drills (see Chapter 10) are good tracking and gap-control exercises for the three-on-two.

10 Ways to Stop Your Opponent's Momentum After a Whistle

Dislodge the net.

Change your stick.

Talk to teammates.

Get or ask for a new water bottle.

Point out a divot in the ice to the referee.

Change goalies temporarily.

Skate to the bench during stoppage (forces a change of goalies?).

Point out a hole in the net (real or imagined).

Equipment problem (i.e., loosen pad straps, trapper loose, etc.).

Talk to the referee/linesman.

Playing Long Shots

When shots originate around the blue line, quick and compact tracking skills are necessary. When challenging blue-line shots, be aware of deflections or passes to off-puck players. Gap control with the net is important. Lateral movement requires the goalie to move from side to side in order to keep good net coverage and stay in the shot lane. Avoid straying too far out from the net (poor gap with net), however, or you will have to go too far back to cover it. Defensemen are supposed to clear a view for the goalie, but the goalie must work to track the play. On long shots, a good gap with the net finds the goalie just at the top of the crease.

With shots from the blue line, butterfly and half-butterfly skills are best. The W and Z Drills (see Chapter 10) with butterfly and half-butterfly attempts are good skill drills for long shots.

Screen Shots

Screen shots are those scary situations where the goalie can't even see the puck because of traffic in front of him. When a screen is on, crouching low helps you to get a glimpse of the puck through the forest of legs. Upper bodies cover most of the upper net, so expect the screen shot to be low. In all cases, good positioning is the key. Tracking the play and getting your feet pointing toward the puck (in the shot lane) will maximize net coverage.

When tracking the play during this situation, a keen goalie can see a screen shot coming. How? By following player positions, especially those of off-puck players who are not covered well, you will be able to estimate where the screen shooter is. If you position yourself at the top of the crease, you will have good net coverage. Your save skills should emphasize the lower half of the net. Listen for the crack off the shooter's stick as a clue that a screen shot is coming. Try to use your half-butterfly or butterfly block tools. The half-butterfly straight-legged save with paddle down is also good, but it overcommits to the lower half of the net.

Deflected Shots

A deflection happens when a player—either offensive or defensive—changes a shot's direction with his stick or skate. Deflections are difficult to stop. The goalie must always play the initial shot first. Sometimes, when a deflection seems probable (such as in goal-mouth traffic after a long shot), it is a good idea to check for wide pass plays. At times, the greater danger is from players near the net. To stop a deflection, a goalie must aggressively move toward the threat and into the shot lane of the deflection when the puck is released. Good net and shooter gap control are key. Experienced goalies read the shot and react with lateral speed, agility, and maximum net coverage. These skills take time to develop.

Screen shot: You will need to battle here to find and then not lose sight of the puck. Track the play action by consistently keeping your feet in the shot lane. Keep your lower body square, but bob and weave only your head and shoulders as necessary to find and fix your eyes on the puck. When the shot is taken you may have to use your other senses, too (i.e., hearing) to make an educated guess as to where the puck is coming from in order to maximize net coverage. The butterfly, half butterfly, and half butterfly with paddle down are good tools here.

The half butterfly, the butterfly block, the paddle down, and the two-pad stack are all save skills commonly used to defend against deflections. The W, X, and Z Drills (see Chapter 10) are good exercises for improving gap control and net awareness for deflections.

Slot Shots

These shots come from the high danger zone located between the face-off dots. Anticipation, positioning, and knowledge of player positions are key to stopping these shots. Reflexes surely help, but good technique enhances even catlike reflexes. A goalie who has good tracking skills and off-puck player awareness will not lose time looking for the slot player. Read those slot-pass plays so as to arrive in position on time. "Bang-bang" plays (a quick pass followed by a quick shot) in the slot, which are beautiful from an offensive standpoint, are especially difficult for a goaltender to defend against. Remember, read and react equal S.P.O.T.: Square, Prepared, on Time.

To challenge the shooter during bang-bang slot plays, always move across the shot lane first; then move out to take away more and more

Slot shot: This is where every shooter loves to get the puck on his stick. Go to the shot lane (and to the top of the crease if you have time) and challenge by selecting the proper save to block the net area (e.g., butterfly, half butterfly, and half butterfly with paddle down). Properly tracking this off-puck player will always give you an advantage to get to that shot-lane position S.P.O.T. (square, prepared, and on time).

net. The net must be covered first, then the angle. In other words, get to the middle of the shot lane (square to the shot) and then move out through the crease.

There are various save skills for defending against slot shots. The butterfly block is our first choice. Your paddle-down tool with one skate dug into the ice for puck pursuit is also a good choice. Here's a useful tip: when you've lost sight of the puck in scrambles, whether they follow a slot shot or other attack situation, quickly glance at the players' eyes—they'll be looking at the puck, which will tip you off to the puck's location. The W and X Drills (see Chapter 10) are good ways to practice slot-shot saves.

Rebounds

Stopping the first shot is the goalie's number-one job, but sometimes a rebound results. A rebound provides your opponent with another chance to score. Although we have been preaching rebound control throughout this book, it is not possible to control them all. If you do allow a rebound, you should pursue the puck to maximize net coverage or to clear the puck away.

10 Forms of Abuse You Will Encounter

Parents, fans, and others blaming you for the loss
Players in your crease screening you
Players charging into you when you challenge out of the crease
Players running into you while you are in the crease
Players kicking your skates out from under you
Players shooting at your head
Players dumping you when you field the puck
Players trying to jar pucks loose that you have frozen
Players stopping quickly to try to spray you with snow
Players piling on top of you when you are down

Controlling the puck means either smothering or deflecting it. Smothering the puck includes catching it with the trapper or even dropping your stick and grabbing the puck with your blocker hand (a move introduced by Dominik Hasek). This is the absolute best method of rebound control. The next best method is to deflect the puck from the net so that there is no rebound. Here, the goalie should be pointing at the puck, like an inverted letter "V." Pucks should glance off the goalie away from opposing players.

145

Other forms of rebound control may not be as pretty or precise. If the situation turns desperate, you may need to slide, kick, shove, or whack the puck away. Above all, remember to be active and pursue the puck!

Rebounds are controllable to a large extent. Great goalies seem to have the puck stick to them or deflect harmlessly away. Their technique is successful because: (1) when they make a save, their overall stance is over the puck (pushing the puck down); (2) their stance and reaction is like a wedge, deflecting pucks away from danger; and (3) the body reacts in a controlled and somewhat relaxed way (if it's possible to say so!) so that the puck is deadened on impact: the reaction is to the puck/shot lane, not kicking/pushing back.

To become a good rebound controller, you must repeat the appropriate skills over and over; keep working at it, especially in practice. This can be hard when coaches run drills that send waves of players, leaving no time to practice rebound control. Stopping the puck is difficult; controlling the rebound is even harder.

If you are a coach, make sure your goalies have the chance to hone this skill. And if they don't appear to want to put in the time and effort to become better at this part of their game, make sure you stress to them the important role it plays in the art of goaltending.

9

Goaltender Coaching

On the simplest level, the goaltender's role in a game is to stop pucks. The game of hockey is changing, however, and demands on goalies are increasing. Active input, aggressive play, and team defense are examples of those new demands. In addition, goalies have to deal with faster and more lateral play. Thankfully, today they are better prepared to confront these challenges.

In today's game of hockey, the goaltender must develop at the same rate as—or faster than—his teammates and the team as a whole. A goalie coach is one resource that a team can use to make sure its goaltenders develop at the proper rate.

10 Ways for Coaches and Parents to Praise

Be positive.
Focus on strengths.
Be consistent.
Be realistic.
Be honest.
Give three positives for every negative. Be constructive, not
   destructive.
Provide solutions to problems and criticisms.
Watch and listen.
Involve the goalies in activities.
Bonus: Avoid use of the words "don't," "not," and "no."

For the goalie coach to be an integral part of the staff, he must fully understand the head coach's ideals and methods. The head coach's team-centered message must also reach the goalies. Working within this framework, the goalie coach becomes an important asset for his team. In other words, the goaltending coach must deal not only with development of player skills, but with communication between the coach and the team's goalie squad.

The skills and techniques of a goalie must be continually taught and honed. Off-ice and on-ice training using drills that reflect game situations will develop, maintain, and sharpen skills. Head coaches should try to use on-ice drills for the whole team: scoring drills for forwards are skill drills for goalies. The objective should be to prepare for top-level performance in a game by simulating gamelike tempo. Pressure experienced during practices pushes the goalies to the next level.

There are several ways in which a goalie coach can keep tabs on the players he coaches. For example, he can avail himself of the team's video equipment and use it to identify a goalie's strengths and weaknesses. It is important, however, that such video be used in a constructive fashion—and not to show up or embarrass a player.

Statistics and direct observation are two other ways that patterns in a goalie's play can be detected. The goaltending coach can use these methods to correct flaws, develop strengths, and increase the goalie's active input. But for these methods to work, the goalie coach must communicate well with both the goaltender and the club's coaching staff.

The goalie coach must not only be able to develop an assessment of the goalies' weaknesses and strengths, he must also know the team as a whole. This way, on-ice drills and postpractice exercises can be designed to enhance both goalie performance and team play. Using information from the goaltender coach, the head coach can begin to get an idea of what to expect from his goalies—and how the goalies fit into the team's overall defensive system.

It is vitally important that the goalie coach reinforce the team's coaching philosophy as he teaches the art of goaltending. Head coaches should try to select a goalie coach who is prepared to to do all he can to further the team's overall goals as he develops the goalies. Sometimes a goalie coach must also allocate his time among two, three, or even four goalies. Obviously, this can be a real juggling act, and sometimes problems occur when each goalie thinks he's not getting enough attention. If you are a goalie coach, try to reach out to each of your goalies, and be open with them about your dilemma. This will help them understand your role. Remind them that their attitude will have a lot to do with how much time you invest in them, that you are trying to serve many masters simultaneously (management, the head coach, the other goalies), and that things may not always seem perfectly fair.

If you are a goalie, you may be coached by many different people with differing opinions over the course of a season or your entire career. Your objective as a goalie should be to listen to and try to learn from each of these people. This will enable you to put new tools in your toolbox and sharpen the ones that are already there.

We have coached countless players who have said, "Didn't you know that so-and-so is *my* goalie coach?" They often go on to say, "And he told me to do it *this* way." Sometimes these goalies then put up a mental block and refuse to learn, which is only the goalie's loss. A goalie coach should understand that not all the skills and techniques being taught will fit into the goalie's toolbox. Even when coaches seem to contradict one another, there is no harm in listening to them all and trying what they recommend. There may come a day when some or all of what they tell you comes in handy.

Goalie Coach Criteria

Who should be a goalie coach and what should he do? In this section we offer our opinions of the qualities a goalie coach should have. Realistically, it is difficult to meet all these criteria. Having played goal is not the only criterion for being a successful goalie coach, but it is certainly helpful.

For the purposes of this discussion, we make a distinction between knowing how to coach goaltenders and simply knowing the craft of goaltending. As you'll see, that distinction also describes two very different approaches to coaching.

Knows how to coach goalies	Knows goaltending
Facilitator (helper)	**Imposer (enforcer)**
help find answers	this is the answer
look for solutions	this is the solution
solicit input	this is what you'll do
Guide	**Director**
find a way	this is the way
try this	do it my way
how far with this?	go this far
instruct to strengths/abilities	change your style
Constructive (positive)	**Destructive (negative)**
build confidence	break down confidence
clear progression	unplanned journey
three positive comments for every criticism	never positive, only critical

Knows how to coach goalies	Knows goaltending
Listener (communicate)	**Talker (insensitive)**
at their side	in their face
what does goalie "see"?	this is what I "see"
hearing and seeing	telling and tunnel vision

Goalie Coach's Influence on Goalies

Goaltenders are often considered loners playing a team sport. Often it seems as if they just wait around for plays to develop and then merely react. This is not entirely wrong. "Don't make the first move" still echoes through every rink today. But we believe that motto can be improved by adding ". . . but be the first in position."

For today's goaltenders, the game involves more than just stopping pucks. As we've stressed over and over, goaltenders must be active members of the overall team game. Consequently, the goalie has to be aware of the team's systems and strategies.

10 Sources of Input for Improvement

150

Goalie coach
Head coach
Assistant coach
Scout
Self (video; self-evaluations)
Parent
Referee
Opposing coaches
Another goalie or teammates
Spectator/friend

The head coach delivers and reinforces the team concept in team meetings, discussions with individual players, in the locker room between periods, and so on. The goaltender coach can be the advocate that a goaltender can relate to as he attempts to incorporate the team message into his own game. A strong relationship may develop between the goalie coach and goalie—especially if the coach is a former goalie who has had similar experiences.

Specific activities of the goalie coach include statistical assessment of a goaltender's game: goals against, shots against, saves, and a variety of other statistics. Goaltending statistics often show patterns of bad play, but a team doesn't want to write off a player—it wants to develop its assets. That is the job of the goalie coach.

The goaltender's inclusion (both mentally and physically) within the framework of the team's strategic concepts (breakouts, penalty killing, D-zone system, game situations, etc.) is another of the goalie coach's areas of responsibility. Positive reinforcement, drill design and execution (for problem resolution), drill selection (for game simulation), and, above all, ensuring two-way communication between the goalie and head coach are other ways that the goalie coach can influence the goaltender and his development.

An important intangible part of the goalie's game is his ability to react to pressure, which can come from his teammates, the head coach, the opposition, his family, and even himself. How does he react to a bad goal? What about last-minute game situations: Does he take charge or wait for things to happen? Does his active input help or hinder the team? The goalie coach can help determine whether the goalie has what it takes to handle pressure and continue to learn and improve. Sometimes the mere presence of the goalie coach serves to reassure the goalie, minimizing the negative effects of pressure.

151

10 Important Mental Attributes for a Goalie

Concentration and focus

Invincibility—competitiveness and stick-to-itiveness

Memory control ("park" or forget poor results, decisions, etc.)

Game sense

Sense of humor

Willingness to learn and to accept constructive criticism

Self-motivation

Good communication

Passion for the game

Desire not to get beat (grit and determination)

Head Coach's Influence on Goalies

Naturally, a head coach has a strong influence on his team, including the goaltenders. If you are a head coach, you know that how your team reacts to game situations influences a goaltender's play, and vice versa. And, as you well know, these mutual reactions determine how successful the team as a whole will be.

The head coach's role in designing practice sessions is a vitally important part of his job. Drills for team practice must involve *all* players, including the goaltender—especially if there are time and space restrictions on the practice ice. The team's goaltenders should be challenged during drills to demonstrate active input. By participating in breakouts, penalty killing, and other game situations, for example, the goaltender can learn the total game by actually seeing it. The goalie must be encouraged to see the big picture of a game situation, not just the puck.

If you are a head coach, get your goaltenders involved in team play. Don't allow them to wander off during team meetings. A goalie must know how his team plays in every game situation. Proactive play and active input are effective only if the goalie and players know what one another are doing. A good motto for goaltenders is "Think like a skater and play like a goalie."

10 Cutting Criticisms You're Bound to Hear Sometime

He lost the game for us.

He let in a soft goal.

He's not a good athlete. (He's too slow.)

He doesn't work hard.

He doesn't focus. (He loses concentration.)

He doesn't want to learn.

If we only had a goalie . . . (He's scared of the puck.)

He can't handle pressure.

He's the coach's favorite.

He doesn't accept criticism.

Pulling the Goalie

Generally, we feel that there are several situations that warrant pulling a goalie at this level of competition. First, if the goalie has shown a lack of focus, it is best to try to let him battle through this for a goal or two. To send a message, however, you might pull him temporarily, talk to him, and then put him back in. Second, regardless of the level of competition, if your goalie throws a temper tantrum, remove him immediately. If he regains his composure on the bench, then you might consider putting him back in. Third, if the team goes down by three goals, you may want to change the goalie, not necessarily because it is his fault but to reprimand and refocus the team and try to change the momentum. Finally, if you are trailing badly and have another game in the next few days, you may want to insert the goalie who is scheduled to start the next game to get him a little bit of work ahead of time. In any case, explain to the goalie your decision to pull him. If need be, give him time to cool off, but do talk to him.

Goalies hurt when they are pulled from a game, but when they feel part of the team, they are more receptive to explanations. As we've seen, one of a coach's main jobs is to involve the team's goalies in the team plan. If you are a coach, design your drills to reflect team needs. Include the goalies—don't just leave them to stand around and wait. Inclusion leads to a sense of contribution.

Provide Positive Reinforcement

Certain catchwords and phrases conjure up specific images and achieve certain objectives. Used properly, these phrases can reinforce your goaltender's mental training during practice. Phrases such as "visualize success" and "image the play" can prepare the goalie for a game. These phrases plant seeds of success and can instill confidence and composure, especially in high-pressure game situations. "See yourself succeed" is another strong mental tool for goaltenders.

153

Game situations allow little time for deliberation—on the ice, it's read and react! During practice, therefore, phrases directly related to success in game situations are excellent reinforcers. When the goalie needs help refocusing or finding composure, these phrases recapture images of success from his experiences.

28 Catchphrases for Positive Reinforcement

Compact economy of motion saves time.
Your hands and upper body must move independently of your legs.
Don't let them score—make them earn it.
Make your challenges efficient; otherwise, there are diminishing returns.
The less you do, the faster and more effective you are.
Trust your instincts.
Track the play, keeping your shoulders, hands, and feet square in the shot lane.
Keep your head on a swivel, tracking the play and seeing off-puck players.

28 Catchphrases for Positive Reinforcement (continued)

A skating goalie is past the point of recovery, off balance, and out of the play.

Have fast feet: fast starts and fast stops.

Where's the puck, where's the post, where am I?

Lead with the stick to the spot where you are going.

Active input: work the game, don't let it work you.

Talk—your defensemen's ears rely on your eyes.

Gap control: control the gap with the net and the gap with the shooter.

On-ice position determines *if* the save is made; style determines *how* the save is made.

Three important basics for save skills: position, position, position.

Think like a player, play like a goalie.

Try to never lose sight of the puck; but if you do, find it fast!

Focus on the puck, but see the whole play.

Anticipate the attack better than the attackers do.

Get to the S.P.O.T.: **s**quare, **p**repared, **o**n **t**ime.

Get to the shot lane.

Recoveries: square up, line up, pop up.

You're good—just play; you'll play well.

Unnecessary overuse of a skill makes you predictable.

Luck is preparation meeting opportunity.

Goaltending's three step rules: get to the shot lane, maximize net coverage, use a specific skill.

Challenges Faced by Goalies and Their Coaches

The goalie's challenge: the goaltender must technically, tactically, and strategically make the transition from practice to game. If practices don't reflect enough gamelike situations, the step from being a good practice goalie to being a good game goalie is very difficult to make.

The coach's challenge: As a coach, plan your practice to reflect your team needs. Remember that team success depends on solid, consistent goaltending. Even the best team can't defend against poor goaltending! Provide challenging practice sessions that involve save technique and team skills to prepare your goaltender. A simple mental reinforcement, such as "where's the puck, where's the post, where am I?" can be enough to adjust on-ice positioning. Encourage the goalie to write the catchphrase you use. Like good golfers, goalies need to pick up on subtleties that help to reinforce, adjust, and improve. These can be retrieved later for refocusing and dealing with pressure.

Coaches can also benefit from having a goalie coach. Coaches must be prepared to understand the developmental needs of their goalies—and make sure that the goalie coach will be an asset to his coaching staff and develop the goaltenders. Goalie coaches who teach the wrong skills or do little to further the team concept are detrimental to the team.

Coaches should avoid the cliche "Goalies just stop pucks." Goalies must be seen as strong, agile athletes, grounded in team concepts. Above all, coaches, goalies are not targets.

At the beginning of this book, the goaltending position was described as the most difficult in hockey. It is also a difficult position to understand. There are many challenges coming at goalies from all sides. In the first place, mustering the courage and executing the skill to stop a puck is a difficult task. On top of this, outside pressures can and will rob the goalie of his powers of concentration. They must be ignored.

Concentration—there's that word again. It is often overused. We feel that the word "concentrate," spoken to goaltenders, only seems to cause more confusion. We prefer the terms "focus" or "be in the game" or "feel the tempo." A goalie must concentrate, but in a manner that allows his motor skills to react quickly and precisely. "Concentrate" seems to imply "think harder." What we mean by staying "focused" is drawing a bead on the action and keeping all distractions out of the picture.

155

At the youth level, of course, we don't expect as much focus from goaltenders as we do at higher levels. Surely, we can't expect an eight-year-old to have the same attention span a fourteen-year-old, as any parent or schoolteacher will attest. However, we can expect a certain amount of discipline. Goaltending requires much discipline—and quite often this takes the form of self-discipline, because goalies don't come to the bench between shifts.

Being a good goalie requires that you master many skills. The toughest skill, however, is not physical—it's mental. For athletes who aspire to reach the top echelons of their sport, the real hurdle in making their bodies perform well is mental discipline. It has been said that the mind is the final frontier; nowhere is this more true than between the pipes in a hockey game, where high levels of discipline and self-control are critical to success. At game time, many goalies tend to grow tense and lock up (concentrating *too* much?); relaxed, focused energy is needed. The goalie needs to achieve a calmness that allows his skills to be unaffected by outside influences or distractions.

A coach can be instrumental in showing how practical, learned skills can be used to attain this discipline. The coach must realize that the pressures on a goalie are many—they come from teammates, coaches, opposing players, the backup goalie, and off-ice problems, to name a few. We speak from experience when we say that these factors do affect the goalie and can influence the goalie's play.

Even at the youth level, competition is intense; but a youngster's natural instinct is to just have fun and play the game—this is as it should be. Coaches must always consider the level at which their team plays. Unnecessary pressure put on a goalie will push that goalie away from the game. Winning is important. But when a youngster quits the game because of pressure to win, everybody loses.

Positive reinforcement is the best approach, particularly at the youth level. Generally, a positive outlook helps a goalie overcome obstacles. Therefore, a coach's constructive criticism should always be accompanied by an acknowledgment of the positive points in the goalie's development.

It has often been said, mostly by coaches and older goalies, that goaltending is 80 percent self-confidence. We agree. For example, a goalie needs a strong level of self-assuredness to overcome assaults on the ego like a soft goal, a heckling fan, or teammates' lack of confidence in him. The goalie must be able to withstand these events that chip away at his confidence.

At the youth level, teammates can often be brutally honest (not to mention brutally cruel). A coach at this level must be able to sense these moments. A youth goalie with good self-confidence should be able to shake off verbal attacks made by teammates on the goalie's play. If he can't, this is where a coach can help. These can be tough moments for both the goalie and coach, and they can sometimes turn into a tough juggling act of egos.

Technique and skills can be learned and practiced. The goalie's real challenge is being able to use the right techniques and skills at the right moment to stifle his opponents. This requires confidence. Mastery occurs when a goalie's mind fires clear, precise messages for reacting in a difficult game situation. There is no fear, no hesitation—just confidence that you are doing the right thing. Whatever the result, learn and improve from it. Skills and technique are the building blocks for being a good goalie. A great work ethic and strong self-confidence will bring you to the top level: recognition as a goalie who can determine the outcome of a game.

One final note: if you want your team to play hard in front of you, you should try to be the most encouraging, prepared, serious, and team-oriented player you can be. Work hard in practice for your team, and your team will work hard for you in the game.

Evaluation Forms

To enable you to systematically chart and analyze your performance, we have developed several evaluation forms. The first, Form 1, should be completed over the course of the game. A coach, backup goalie, parent, or other observer can record the situation and placement for each of the goals scored against both teams.

Form 2 should be completed after each game. At the very least, you should do it for your own goalie(s). Roll the information from Form 1 into a summary for the game, looking for patterns with regard to the situations leading to and placements of each of the goals scored, both for and against your team. This form also enables you to calculate and record a number of relevant statistics. Copies of these forms should be kept on file so that they can be used to prepare for the next game against the same opponent. More important, you may face this opponent in the playoffs, and knowing its goalies' tendencies could prove to be valuable. Finally, some teams have networks set up to exchange information pertaining to common opponents, and this is one very important, desirable input.

Form 3 should be completed periodically over the course of the season. Most NHL teams break their seasons down into ten-game segments. You should prepare this form for each of your goalies. Roll the information from Form 2 into a summary for the segment, looking for patterns with regard to the situations leading to and placements of each of the goals scored against the goalies. This form also enables you to record a number of relevant statistics.

Form 4 provides you with a comprehensive document that can be used to evaluate a developing goalie. It captures all of the components covered in this book. You can have multiple observers fill it out, provided they are qualified. These forms should be reviewed throughout the current year and retained by the goalie for use in later years. The last part of the form should be used to set goals and objectives for improvement. If your goalie can improve three to four tools per year, he will become a complete goalie within a few short years.

The Hockey Goalie's Handbook © 2002
Jim Corsi and John Hannon, Ph.D.

FORM 1: GOAL BY GOAL REPORT

DATE: _____

TEAMS: **(A)** _____ **@ (H)** _____
GOALIES: **(A)** _____ **@ (H)** _____
(A) _____ **@ (H)** _____

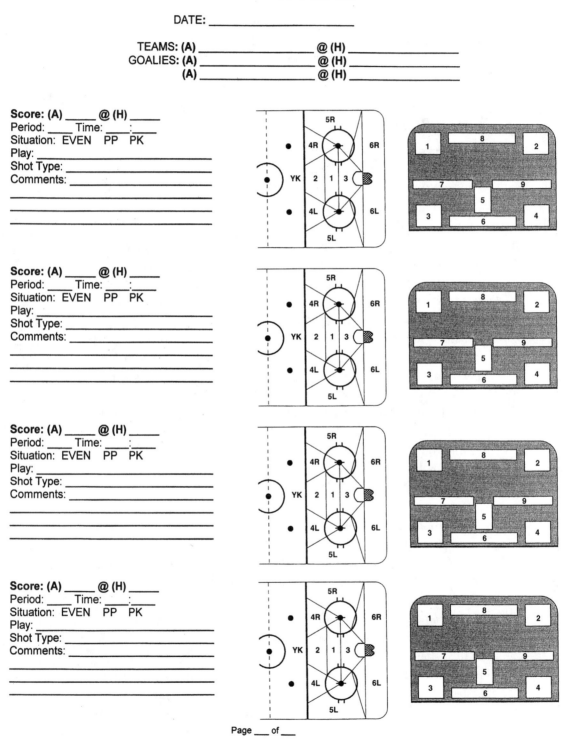

Score: (A) _____ **@ (H)** _____
Period: ____ Time: ____:____
Situation: EVEN PP PK
Play: _____
Shot Type: _____
Comments: _____
_____
_____
_____

Score: (A) _____ **@ (H)** _____
Period: ____ Time: ____:____
Situation: EVEN PP PK
Play: _____
Shot Type: _____
Comments: _____
_____
_____
_____

Score: (A) _____ **@ (H)** _____
Period: ____ Time: ____:____
Situation: EVEN PP PK
Play: _____
Shot Type: _____
Comments: _____
_____
_____
_____

Score: (A) _____ **@ (H)** _____
Period: ____ Time: ____:____
Situation: EVEN PP PK
Play: _____
Shot Type: _____
Comments: _____
_____
_____
_____

The Hockey Goalie's Handbook © 2002
Jim Corsi and John Hannon, Ph.D.

FORM 2: POST GAME REPORT

DATE: _____

TEAMS: **(A)** _____ @ **(H)** _____
GOALIES: **(A)** _____ @ **(H)** _____
(A) _____ @ **(H)** _____
FINAL SCORE: **(A)** _____ @ **(H)** _____

NAME OF OUR GOALIE(S)

SHOTS ON GOAL _____ : 1) ____ 2) ____ 3) ____ OT) ____ TOTAL) ____
SHOTS ON GOAL _____ : 1) ____ 2) ____ 3) ____ OT) ____ TOTAL) ____

CHANCES _____ : 1) ____ 2) ____ 3) ____ OT) ____ TOTAL) ____
CHANCES _____ : 1) ____ 2) ____ 3) ____ OT) ____ TOTAL) ____

GOALS AGAINST _____ : 1) ____ 2) ____ 3) ____ OT) ____ TOTAL) ____
GOALS AGAINST _____ : 1) ____ 2) ____ 3) ____ OT) ____ TOTAL) ____

NAME OF OUR GOALIE(S)

SAVE PERCENTAGE ((SHOTS-GOALS)/SHOTS): _____ ____
SAVE PERCENTAGE ((SHOTS-GOALS)/SHOTS): _____ ____

CHANCE PERCENTAGE ((CHANCES-GOALS)/CHANCES) _____ ____
CHANCE PERCENTAGE ((CHANCES-GOALS)/CHANCES) _____ ____

DECISION IN THIS GAME: **OUR GOALIE:** _____ Win Loss Tie
OUR GOALIE: _____ Win Loss Tie

RECORD FOR OUR GOALIE _____ : Wins ____ Losses ____ Ties ____
RECORD FOR OUR GOALIE _____ : Wins ____ Losses ____ Ties ____

PATTERNS OF GOALS SCORED FOR THIS GAME

Goals Scored in Rink Location

1	2	3	4L	4R	5L	5R	6L	6R	YK

Goals Scored in Net Location

1	2	3	4	5	6	7	8	9

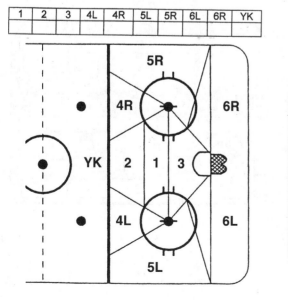

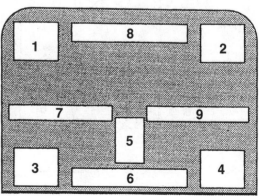

The Hockey Goalie's Handbook © 2002
Jim Corsi and John Hannon, Ph.D.

FORM 3: SEGMENT REPORT

From _____ to _____

NAME OF OUR GOALIE: _____

Team											
Date											Totals
Shots											
Chances											
Goals											
W											
L											
T											

SAVE PERCENTAGE ((SHOTS-GOALS)/SHOTS):   ____

CHANCE PERCENTAGE ((CHANCES-GOALS)/CHANCES)   ____

RECORD FOR OUR TEAM IN THIS SEGMENT: Wins ____   Losses ____   Ties ____

RECORD FOR OUR GOALIE IN THIS SEGMENT: Wins ____   Losses ____   Ties ____

PATTERNS OF GOALS SCORED FOR THIS GAME

 # Goals Scored in Rink Location

1	2	3	4L	4R	5L	5R	6L	6R	YK

 # Goals Scored in Net Location

1	2	3	4	5	6	7	8	9

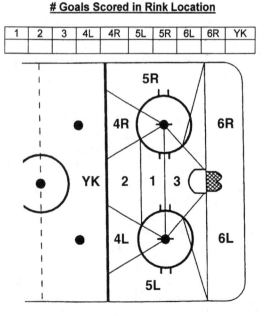

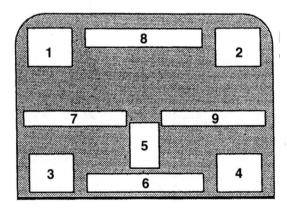

The Hockey Goalie's Handbook © 2002
Jim Corsi and John Hannon, Ph.D.

FORM 4: YOUTH GOALIE EVALUATION
DATE OF EVALUATION: _____

Name: _____ Nickname _____ Male Female

Date of Birth: _____ Years playing goal: _____ Team: _____

Age Group (e.g. Pee-Wee) : _____ Level (e.g. House, A, AA, AAA): _____

RATING SCALE
Compared to peers in same Age Group and Level (i.e., Pee-Wee AAA)

5. Far Above Average	4. Above Average	3. Average	2. Below Average	1. Far Below Average

Ready Stance	Rating	Comments
Presentation		
Balance		
Crouch		
Hands		
Stick		
Recovery		

Skating	Rating	Comments
Forward		
Forward T-glide		
Forward Stop		
Backward		
Backward Stop		
Telescoping		
Lateral Shuffle		

Movement	Rating	Comments
Quickness		
Compactness		
Upper/Lower Independence		

FORM 4: YOUTH GOALTENDER EVALUATION (Page 2)

Save Techniques	Rating	Comments
Trapper Saves		
Blocker Saves		
Blocker/Trapper Combination		
Arm Saves		
Chest Saves		
Skate Saves – Trapper Side		
Skate Saves – Blocker Side		
Skate & Stick Combination		
½ Butterfly – Trapper Side		
½ Butterfly – Blocker Side		
Full Butterfly Saves		
Stack Pads Saves		
Knee/Thigh Saves		
Stick Saves		
Stick Checks		
Paddle-Down Saves		
Puckhandling		
Net Awareness		
Tracking		
Angles		
Player Positioning		

FORM 4: YOUTH GOALTENDER EVALUATION (Page 3)

Game Situations	Rating	Comments
Tracking Play Action		
Going to Shot Lane		
Staying Square in Shot Lane		
Breakaways (2:0, 1:0)		
Even Man Rushes (1:1, 2:2)		
Odd Man Rushes (2:1, 3:2)		
Long Shots		
Screen Shots		
Deflected Shots		
Slot Shots		
Rebounds		
Communication		
Active Input		

Competitiveness	Rating	Comments
Practice Work Ethic		
Game Intensity		
Respected by Coaches		
Respected by Teammates		
Passion for The Game		

TARGETED IMPROVEMENT AREAS   **ACTION PLANS**

1. _____   _____

2. _____   _____

3. _____   _____

4. _____   _____

10

Drills

Generally, practice is centered on skating, passing, stick handling, team play and so on. The goaltenders' skills are practiced passively—that is, most of the team's drills end up with a shot at the goalie. In view of the team's overall composition, this seems fair. Why work on the goalies' skills and needs when there are only two of them, at most, and 18 skaters?

However, most knowledgeable hockey people will tell you that the goaltenders' team value can be 60 percent or more! Surely, then, team-training sessions should involve a lot of shots that allow the goalie to practice his skills. In fact, most practices involve too much routine shooting.

A goalie's weak points are seldom tested adequately in team drills. And when a situation in which the goalie can learn occurs, it is usually so fleeting that the goalie may not learn anything—and may surrender a goal to boot.

But let's not lose our proper perspective regarding team sports that involve goaltending. There is only a limited amount of practice time (at the amateur level, at least); hence, practice cannot be dedicated to developing the goalies' skills. That's why we have come up with some solutions for the hockey goaltender starved for attention while his team practices.

First, it is important that the goalkeeper's weaknesses are clearly understood. For young goaltenders, those weaknesses may be attributable to a wide range of causes, such as lack of strength, fear of injury, poor equipment, or weak game knowledge. However, when drills are set up to work on weak areas, failure to improve from drills can be discouraging. Inexperienced or young athletes see their weaknesses highlighted as these drills expose their vulnerability. This is where a cooperative and patient coach can help the athlete improve. Weaknesses can be overcome by practicing the proper motions (repetition) or by developing other skills so that the weaknesses are rarely exposed (substitution). However, all this will be for naught if the coach neglects to properly identify the goalie's strengths and weaknesses.

10 Things to Do If You Are Ignored in Practice

Up/Downs
W, X, Y, and Z skating drills
Sprints
Post touches (behind-the-net net play action)
Puck handling
Watching closely and quietly
Fielding pucks behind the net
Switching with the other goalie
Communicating with teammates
Simulating save skills

For a goalie to remain confident in his abilities, he needs encouragement from his instructors and coaches. As much as possible, a coach should use positive reinforcement—and avoid "don't" and other negative words. The coach should strive for a ratio of two or three praises for every criticism. We are not saying that a player should be babied. But the fact is that many young players, goalies included, get turned off to the game and drop it when they lose confidence in their ability. Always be conscious of the player's skill level before making demands.

Practices, both on and off the ice, should reflect the level (speed, strength, precision) of play encountered in actual games. Drills that work on team skills ending with a play action to the goal give the goaltender the opportunity to practice game situations. Defensemen and attackers should play at high tempo. This increases demands on the goalie's reaction time, speed of decision making, and overall play.

Of course, play actions reflecting game situations train the whole team. At times, it is not easy to be goalie-specific. At the pro level, practice time is difficult to find because there are so many games in the schedule. This means that training specific to goalkeepers is even more difficult to accomplish during practices. Good coaches realize this and run practices at a high tempo, which is preparation in itself for goaltenders. Occasionally, a half-ice drill leaves room for goalie-specific training at the other end of the rink. If not, there is some-

KID'S KEY: PRACTICES

- Work on net awareness (W, X, Y, and Z) drills if you are being ignored.
- Try your hardest to stop each and every puck.
- Understand the entire drill—don't just wait for the shot.

times time at the end of practice to work on techniques and skills with proper drills.

Drill to Skill

- The on-ice activity is where we try giving players opportunities to learn, improve, and perfect—that is, "drill to skill."
- When selecting or preparing drills, try to think about (1) scoring chances that reflect game situations, (2) save skill focus, and (3) timing.
- Progressions should be set based on skill level and time constraints; a good step-by-step process, for example, is (1) still puck, (2) moving puck, (3) moving player, (4) moving puck and player, (5) moving puck, player, and goalie.
- Explain to shooters that drills are scoring drills. Explain to goalies that drills are goalie drills.

- When trying to promote change, remember that the process may involve *undoing* by *doing* positive drills/exercises.
- Strengthening good skills will promote change, especially when the goalie's confidence builds in the process.
- Remember that when goalies, especially young and developing goalies, start to tire or lose confidence, they may well revert to old habits and/or retreat deeper into the net than they usually would. This is normal—until the old habit becomes the good old habit. That's the difference between average goaltending and good, solid goaltending.

Generally, drills should be performed under a set of guidelines:
Duration—45 seconds to 1 minute, 30 seconds per repetition
Repetitions—2 or 3, depending on skill level or intensity
Reset—Allow a work-to-rest ratio of 1:2 (drill for one minute, rest for two minutes, repeat)
Workup—Increase or decrease as skill and/or strength requires

Key to Skating and Shooting Drills

 Skating direction

Skating direction carrying puck

 Backward skating

Ⓖ Goaltender

② Shooter/player

Shot

△ Pylon

| Obstacle

Jump over obstacle

Skating Drills

W Drill (Skating)

1 minute, or repeat 2 times
Start/repeat/return

Sequence

1. Start at left post
2. Forward skate and stop left foot; backward return to left post
3. Forward skate center and stop left foot; backward return to right post
4. Forward skate and stop right foot; backward return to right post
5. Reverse (start on right post)
6. Repeat

Key Points

- Offensive-zone tracking
- Low to high tracking
- Power play
- At (2), (3), (4), simulate save skill (optional)

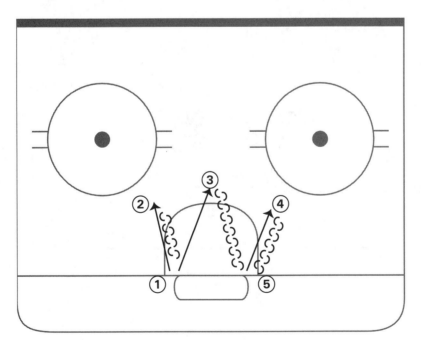

X Drill (Skating)

1 minute, or repeat 2 times

Sequence

1. Start on left post
2. Forward skate and stop left foot
3. Backward: 1 or 2 cuts and T-push/shuffle to right post
4. Forward skate and stop right foot
5. Backward: 1 or 2 C-cuts and T-push or shuffle to left post
6. Reverse
7. Repeat

Key Points

- Behind-the-net tracking
- Point-to-point plays
- Odd-man rushes
- Add save simulations to drill at each post and (2) and (4) (optional)

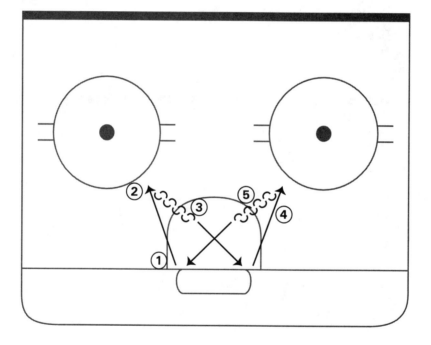

Y Drill (Skating)

1 minute, or repeat 2 times

Sequence

1. Start at left post
2. Forward to center
3. Forward through slot and T-stop
4. Backward through slot: 1 or 2 C-cuts
5. T-push or shuffle to right post
6. Reverse
7. Repeat

Key Points

- Breakaway
- At-net drives
- Add save simulations to drill at (1), (3), (5)

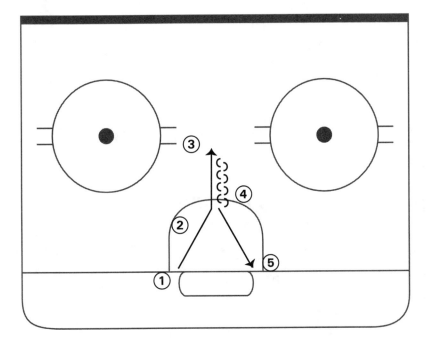

Z Drill (Skating)

1 minute, or repeat 2 times

Sequence

1. Start at left post
2. Shuffle right to right post
3. Forward skate left side; T-push
4. Shuffle right across top of crease
5. Backward return to right post
6. Reverse
7. Repeat

Key Points

- Behind-the-net tracking
- Point shot
- Low-to-high tracking
- Add save simulations to drill at each post and (4) and (5)

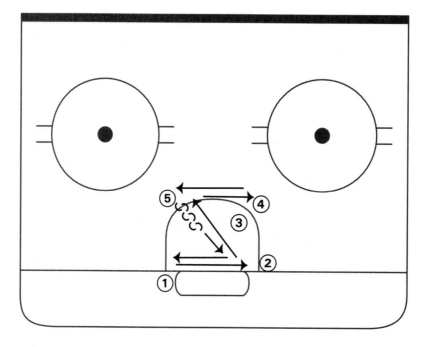

172

Inside Edge Start-and-Stop Drill

1 minute, or left then right

Sequence

1. Start in corner on goal line; skate forward in ready stance
2. Face same direction for all stops:
   left foot—(2) (4) (6) (8) (10) stop by using inside edge
   Right foot—(3) (5) (7) (9) (11)
3. Reverse
4. Repeat

Key Points

- Fast feet
- Maintain stance
- Keep hands steady while skating
- Upper body independent of lower body

173

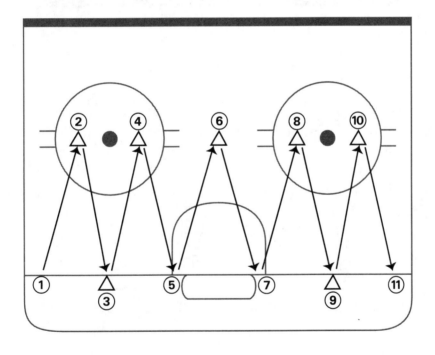

Shuffle Drill

1 minute, or left then right

Sequence

1. Start in corner on goal line; sideways shuffle
2. Face same direction for all stops:
   left foot—(2) (4) (6) (8) (10)
   right foot—(3) (5) (7) (9) (11)
   stop by using inside edge
3. Reverse
4. Repeat

Key Points

- Compact movement
- Maintain stance
- Edge awareness
- Fast feet
- Keep stick facing forward
- Stop by using inside edge

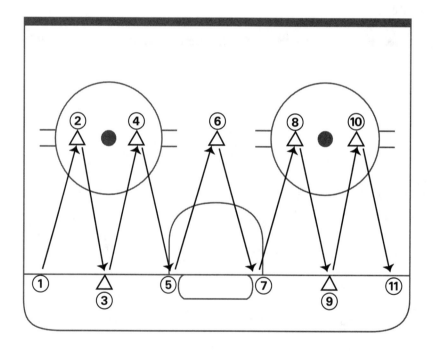

T-Glide (Lateral) Drill

1 minute, or left then right

Sequence

1. Start in corner on goal line; skate laterally using T-glide/T-push
2. Face same direction for all stops:
   left foot—(2) (4) (6) (8) (10)
   right foot—(3) (5) (7) (9) (11)
   stop by using inside edge of leading foot
3. Reverse (use other foot)
4. Repeat

[art 10-106]

Key Points

- Compact movement
- Maintain stance
- Edge awareness
- Keep stick facing forward
- No bobbing up and down

175

Backward Drill

1 minute, or left then right

Sequence

1. Start in corner on goal line; backward in ready stance
2. Look over right shoulder moving to (2), (4), (6), (8), (10)
3. Look over left shoulder moving to (3), (5), (7), (9), (11)
4. T-stop, turn, and continue backward
5. Reverse
6. Repeat

Key Points

- Compact movement
- Maintain stance
- Keep hands steady
- Practice looking over one shoulder while skating backward

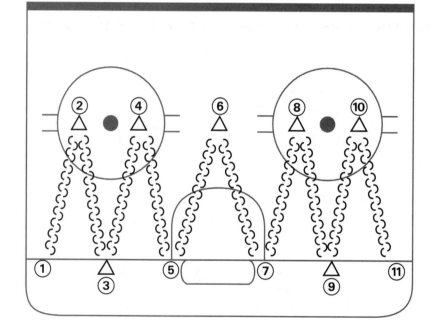

Telescoping Drill

1 minute, or left then right

Sequence

1. Start in corner on goal line; forward in ready stance using T-push left foot
2. Stop, then backward in ready stance
3. Stop, forward in ready stance using T-push left foot—face far end of rink throughout
4. Reverse (use T-push right foot going forward)
5. Repeat

Note: While skating backward, look over appropriate shoulder.

Key Points

- Quick transitions
- Maintain stance
- Pivot forward/backward/ forward
- Edge control
- Avoid bobbing up and down during pivot/transition

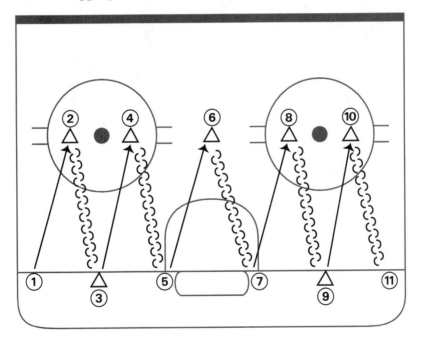

Telescoping with Save Drill

1 minute, or left then right

Sequence

Add save simulations to telescoping at X: full butterfly, half butterfly, smother, 2-pad slide, paddle down

Note: After forward skating, stop and make save. (See Telescoping Drill for skating details.)

Key Points

- Quick transitions
- Visualization
- Muscle memory
- Recovery
- Gap control

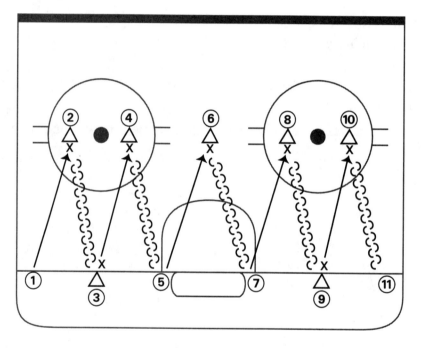

Iron Cross Drill

1 minute, or once through drill (goalie position throughout)

Sequence

Done within a circle or in large area as shown

1. Forward (T-push)
2. Backward
3. Shuffle right
4. Shuffle left
5. Backward
6. Forward
7. T-glide left with right foot push
8. T-glide right with left foot push
9. Repeat or continue 2 or 3 times as conditioning improves

Key Points

- Quick transitions
- Fast feet
- Compact, steady stance
- Avoid bobbing up and down
- Edge control
- Quick stops and starts
- Conditioning

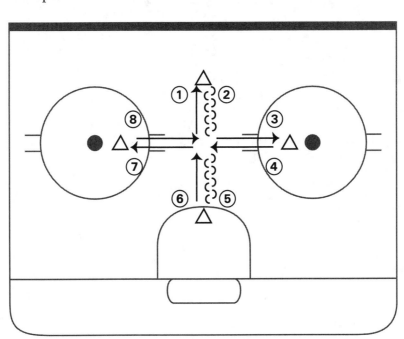

Iron Cross with Save Drill
(see Iron Cross Drill for skating details)

1 minute, or once through drill (goalie position while skating)

Sequence

Add save simulations to iron cross at X: full butterfly, half butterfly, smother, paddle down, 2-pad slide

Key Points

- Quick transitions
- Visualization
- Muscle memory
- Recovery
- Skill use during movement
- Forward skating stop, then make save

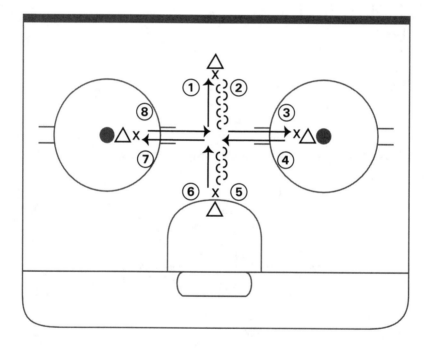

Triple-Skate Drill (forward, backward, lateral)

1 minute, or left then right

Sequence

1. Start in left corner; forward skate in ready stance, T-push
2. Shuffle right
3. Backward skate in ready stance
4. Shuffle right shuffle
5–11. Continue initial sequence
12. Repeat reverse (shuffle left now)

Key Points

- Quick transitions
- Eyes up
- Compact movement
- Upper body independent of lower body
- Alternate T-push lateral for shuffle

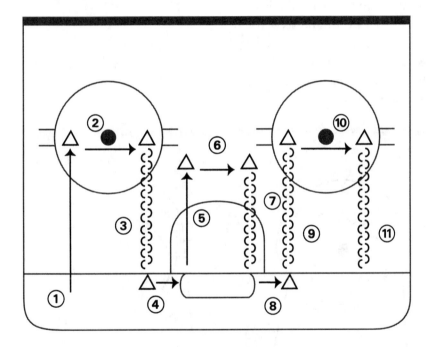

Circles Forward Drill

1 minute, or left then right

Sequence

1. Start in left corner, skate forward
2. Clockwise around first circle 2 times
3. Exit circle and skate to left post
4. Pivot, backward skating away from post
5. Pivot, backward to other post
6. Pivot and forward skating
7. Clockwise around second circle 2 times
8. Exit to corner
9. Reverse (counterclockwise)
10. Repeat

Key Points

- Quick transitions
- Fast feet
- Skating drills
- Conditioning

182

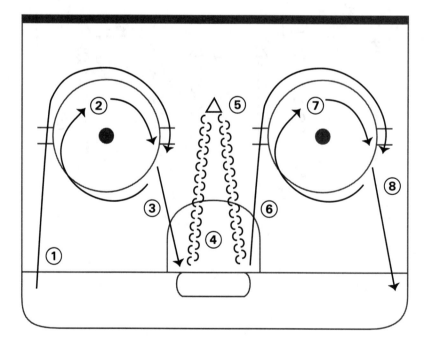

Circles Backward Drill

1 minute, or left then right

Sequence

1. Start in left corner, backward skating
2. Clockwise around first circle 2 times; exit circle and skate to left post
3. Pivot and skate forward—stop
4. Pivot, forward to right post
5. Pivot and backward
6. Clockwise around second circle 2 times and to corner
7. Reverse (counterclockwise)
8. Repeat

Key Points

- Quick transitions
- Fast feet
- Steady stance
- Quick looks over alternate shoulder

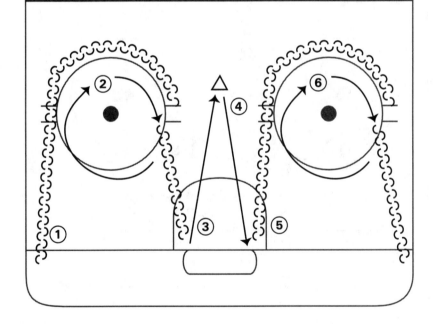

Lateral Stick Jump

1 minute, or left then right
Place 4 sticks (ladderlike) perpendicular
to goal line 6–8 feet apart

Sequence

1. Start on left post; forward skate left, T-push and stop
2. Jump sideways over stick
3. T-push lateral to next stick, left foot push and stop; then jump sideways over stick
4. Repeat
5. Backward to right post; repeat and reverse (right foot T-push)

Key Points

- Fast feet
- Edge control
- Agility
- Stay square
- Add save simulations to drill at stops, before and/or after jumps
- Alternate shufflle for T-push lateral

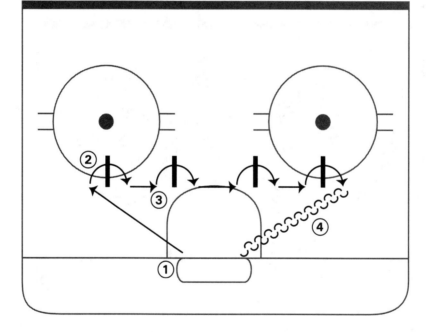

Forward Stick Jump Drill

One time through
Place 3 sticks (ladderlike) parallel to goal line 8–10 feet apart

Sequence

1. Start at left post, forward skate, T-push, and stop
2. Jump forward over stick and stop
3. T-glide forward to next stick, left foot push and stop
4. Continue
5. Shuffle to right; then pivot to backward, "slalom" around pylons to right post

Key Points

- Fast feet
- Agility
- Stay square
- Add save skill simulations to drill at stops, before and/or after jumps

Note: Repeat by placing sticks on right and pylons on left.

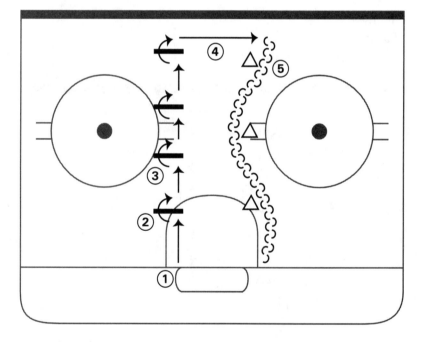

Lateral Stick Jump Drill

One time through
Place 4 sticks in a line perpendicular
to goal line about 3 feet apart

Sequence

1. Start on right post and then forward skate, T-push, and stop
2. Lateral jump left, controlled and stop
3. Forward skate, T-push, and stop
4. Lateral jump right, controlled and stop; continue
5. Shuffle left
6. Backward return to left post, slalom around pylons

Key Points

- Fast feet
- Agility
- Edge control
- Stay square
- Add save simulations to drill at "stops" before and/or after jump

Note: Repeat by placing sticks on left and pylons on right

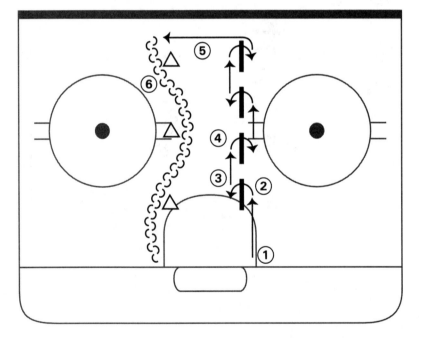

Two-Goalie Fielding Drill

Repetitions vary
One goalie at left post; another at right post

Sequence

1. Sprint to side boards forward
2. Stop, facing up ice
3. Return to post position— 1-2-3 is one cycle
4. Repeat 2 to 5 times as conditioning improves
5. Goalies switch sides
6. Repeat

Key Points

- Speed
- Net awareness
- Add a puck to stick-handle during skating
- Rest between cycles twice the time of one cycle

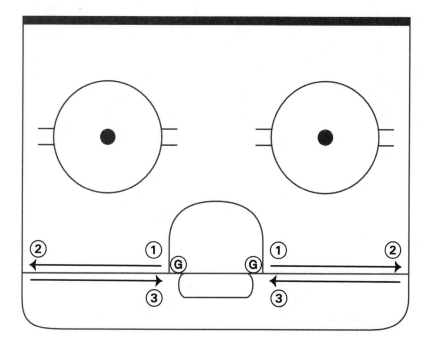

Two-Goalie Retrievals Drill

Repetitions vary
One goalie at left post; another at right post

Sequence

1. Spring to point at boards behind the net
2. Stop and touch board with stick
3. Return to post position
4. Repeat 2 to 5 times as conditioning improves
5. Goalies switch sides
6. Repeat

Key Points

- Urgency (quick stops and starts)
- Fast feet
- Net awareness
- Always facing up ice
- Add pucks behind net at (2) for goalies to clear/pass up the boards

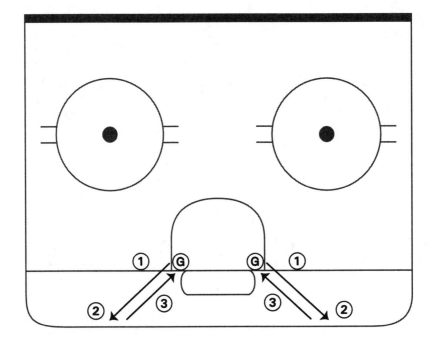

Shooting Drills

The saves skills used in the following drills may vary. Coach and goalie(s) should work together to decide on the practiced skill—for example, on low shots use the half butterfly—or simple stop the puck.

W Drill (Shooting)

Number of pucks varies with skill and conditioning
Add shots to Skating W Drill from shooters at (2), (3), and (5)

Sequence

1. Start at right post and T-push
2. Stop shot from player (2); then backward to right post
3. Forward and out to challenge shot from player (3)
4. Two C-cuts and shuffle/T-glide to left post
5. T-push forward, stop, and challenge shot from player (5)
6. Backward to left post and repeat same, starting at left post

(See Skating W Drill for details.)

Key Points

- Steady hands while skating
- Bring hands to puck for leg saves
- Recover to stance and move to next shot simultaneously
- Lead with stick and check for legs "thrusting" to shot lane

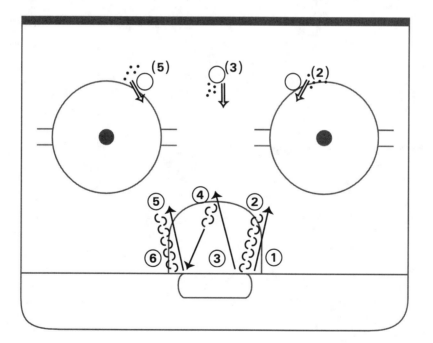

X Drill (Shooting)

4 pucks each shooter
Add shots to X Skating Drill from shooters
at (1), (2), (3), and (4)

Sequence

1. Start at left post and T-push forward to challenge shot from player (1)
2. Two C-cuts; then T-push lateral or shuffle to right post for shot from player (2)
3. Out and challenge (T-push forward) shot from (3): then two C-cuts; then T-push lateral or shuffle to left post for shot from (4)

(See Skating X Drill for details.)

Key Points

- Fast feet
- Bring hands to puck for leg saves
- Recovery to stance and move to next shot simultaneously
- Lead with stick to shot lane
- Skill and conditioning

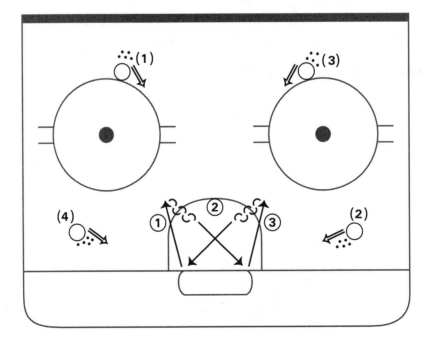

Y Drill and Controlled Deke

Left and right twice

Sequence

1. Start at left post, forward T-push to slot, and stop
2. Stop shot from player (2); then recover to stance
3. Backward two—C-cut thrust (shuffle or T-push) to right post
4. Quick low shot from player (4)
5. Repeat from right post; same: finish with player shot (6)

(See Skating Y Drill for details.)

Key Points

- Fast feet
- Gap control to cover net on "deke"
- Use butterfly, half butterfly, or 2-pad slide to post

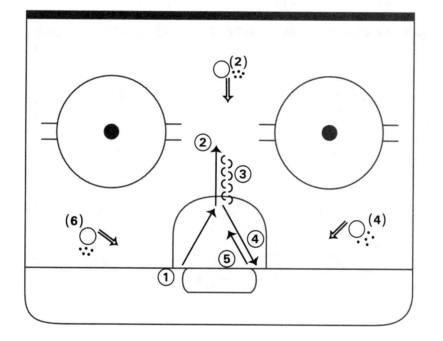

Z Drill with Butterfly Saves

Sequence

1. Shot at left post (stand-up) from player F1 at (1)
2. Shuffle to right post (stand-up) for shot from player F2 at (2)
3. Z Drill; diagonal for challenge from F3 for shot (3)
4. Shuffle right for shot from F4 at (4)
5. Shuffle left for shot from F3 at (3)
6. Repeat sequence starting at right post

(See Skating Z Drill for details.)

Key Points

- At-post net coverage
- Feet on post
- Use T-slide or shuffle from post to post
- Shots at post are from below circle

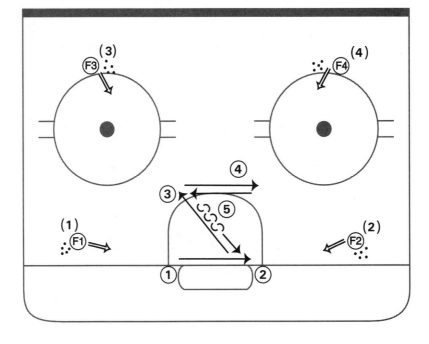

Shuffle Drill with Stick Saves

8-puck drill—4 pucks each at (1) and (2)

Sequence

1. Start at left post, out and stop; shot from player at (1) for stick save
2. Backward to same post
3. Shuffle to right post
4. Out and challenge shot from (2); then backward to same post
5. Continue and repeat

Key Points

- Post-to-post lateral movement
- Stick-save control
- Tracking

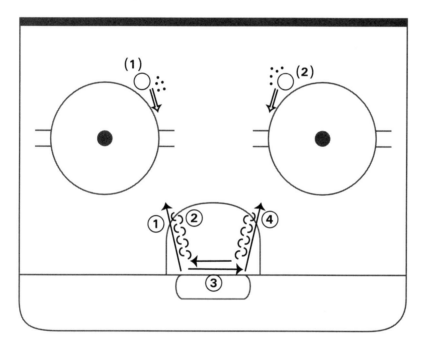

Straight Shuffle with Mixed Saves

10-puck drill—5 pucks each way

Sequence

1. Out, stop to challenge shooter
2. Short/quick shuffle of legs to close 5-hole (fast feet), with 5 quick shots from player (2). Shots are quick and follow lateral motion of goalie (5 pucks each way)
4. Repeat to challenge with same shuffle and shot sequence (other way)

Key Points

- Shuffle short, lateral steps
- Maintain positioning at top of crease or out farther
- Use variety of save skills
- Quickness

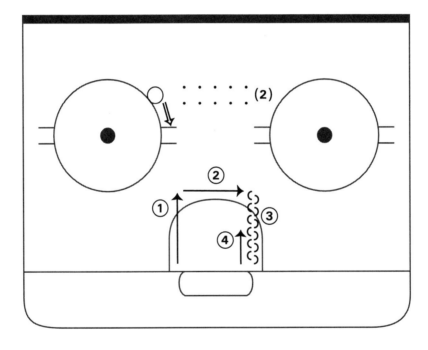

Pretzel Drill

6-puck drill

Sequence

1. On back; up; shot (1)
2. On belly; up; shot (2)
3. Butterfly; up; shot (3)
4. Half butterfly (left leg); up; shot (4)
5. Half butterfly (right leg); up; shot (5)
6. Deke (6)

Key Points

- Recoveries to stance, then shot
- Maintain top of crease during recovery
- Recovery facing puck
- Conditioning

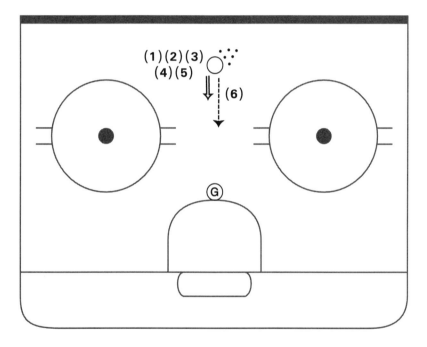

Blocker and Trapper

Left, then right

Sequences

1. Start at post out and transition around pylon
2. Gain position for shot (1) (high to far side)
3. Return (use two C-cuts and then shuffle or T-glide) to opposite post
4. Out, transition, shot (2) (high to far side)
5. Return to opposite and repeat

Key Points

- Foot speed and agility
- Watch puck to gloves
- Hands steady during skating
- High shot to far side for blocker or trapper save skill

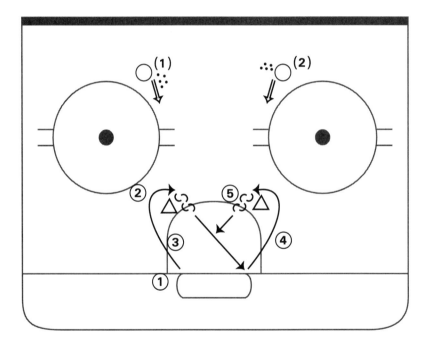

Rebound and Smother

1 minute

Sequence

1. Out from right post, save shot (1)
2. Soft/slow/loose puck (2) for goalie to cover up (second puck from same player)
3. Recover to feet and quickly to left post
4. Out for shot (3) and continue with second puck (4) to other side to cover up
5. Continue

Key Points

- Push puck into ice for smother
- Protect trapper with stick or use paddle-down smother
- High shot to far side for blocker or trapper save skill

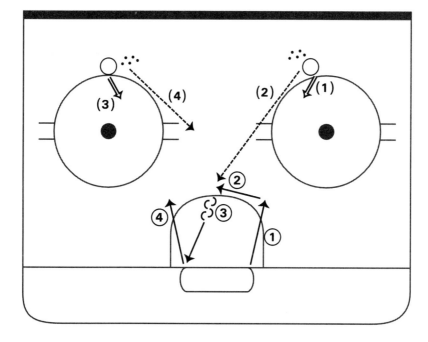

Low-High Wraparound

1 minute

Sequence

1. Rapid-succession shots by players F1 (1); then F2 (2) and F3 for shot (3)
2. Shots from cycle in corners—quick release pivoting around pylon with goalie out to challenge
3. Goalie returns to post for wraparound from F4 (4)
4. Goalie recovers for repeat from same side
5. Continuous/repeat other side

Key Points

- Track, maintaining short-side post of shot lane
- Timing for shooters after wraparound
- Use of paddle down and pursue puck with stick blade

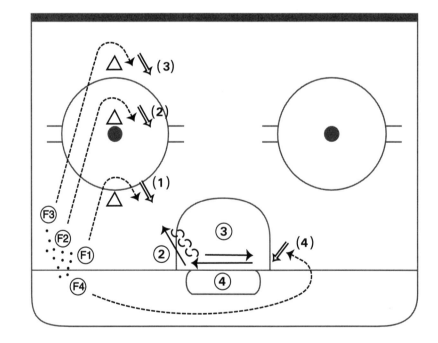

Two Shot/Two Tip

1 minute

Sequence

1. Rapid succession
2. Shots from F1 and F2 out of corners with shots (1), (2)
3. Next player in line then passes to point F3
4. Long shots by F3 (3), (4) with deflect, screen, and rebounds played by F1 and F2, who have moved to front of net
5. Goalie recovers for repeat
6. Continuous/repeat other side

Key Points

- Recoveries
- Track off-puck players
- Rebound control
- Low-to-high tracking from short side

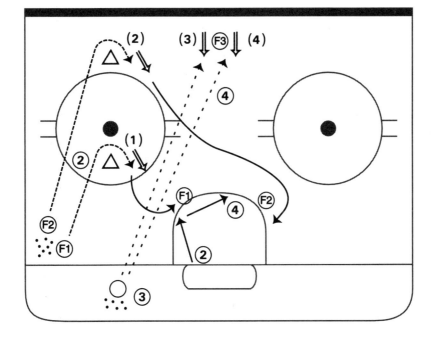

Stack Pad/Butterfly

1 minute

Sequence	Key Points

Sequence

1. Out from left post, stop and make save (1), read pass (2) for stack-pad (or butterfly) save
2. Up and out from right post to challenge shot (3); then read pass-shot (4) for stack-pass (or butterfly) save

Key Points

- Time to recover for new shot
- Recoveries to face new shooter
- Off-puck player awareness
- Stack pad (or butterfly) is square to shot and to the shot lane
- Alternate stack-pad and butterfly save
- Play-action X Drill

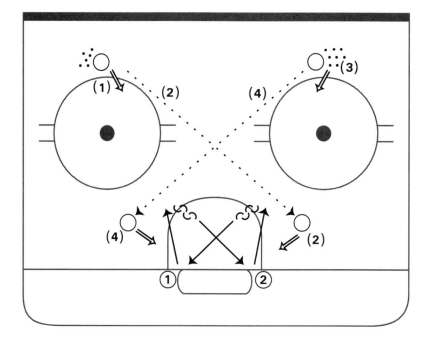

Walkout/Lateral Drive

6 pucks

Sequence

1. 3 pucks each side and stick length away
2. Alternate sides and same shooter
3. Gain net (no higher than pylon) for lateral drive for shots (1), (2), (3), (4), (5), and (6)

Key Points

- Butterfly skills
- Poke-check skills
- Paddle down
- Aggressive puck pursuit, then to shot lane
- Recoveries

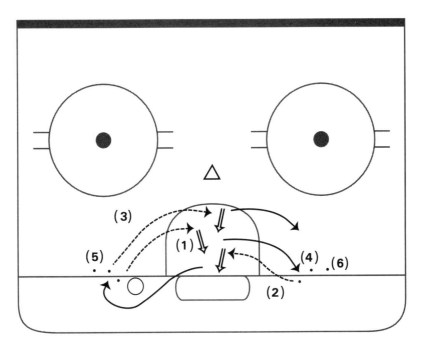

Dekes (controlled)

12 pucks

Sequence

1. Goalie out of crease (Y Drill)
2. Player tries to deke (not shoot) by goalie
3. All 4 pucks (left side) recover after each deke (1), (2), (3), (4)
4. Repeat—4 dekes (right side): (5), (6), (7), (8)
5. Repeat—4 dekes (any side): (9), (10), (11), (12)

Key Points

- Gap control
- Recovery
- Compact, ready stance
- Fast feet
- Conditioning

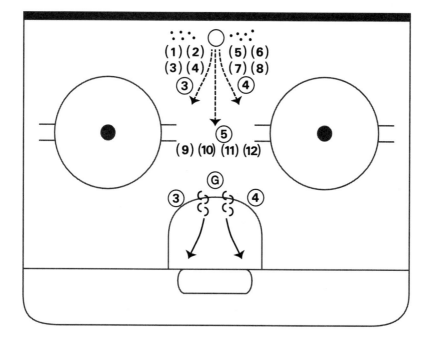

Triple Attack and Lateral Play Action

1 minute

Sequence

1. Shot from wing (1) by player F1
2. Quick (2) shot by F2 to force goalie back (check gap control)
3. F2 after shot, passes (3) to F3 for deke (4)

Key Points

- Off-puck player
- Edge control
- Recovery
- Lateral movement to track pass

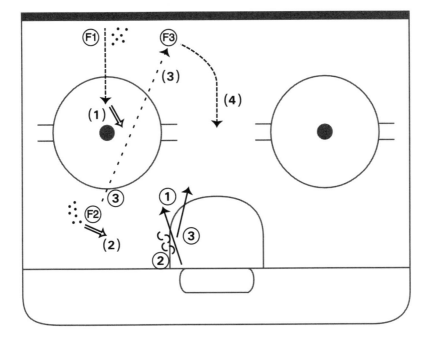

Short Poke Check/Low-High Action

2 minutes

Sequence

1. Player F1 behind net makes pass (1)
2. Goalie tries to short poke check
3. If pass gets through to player F2, play shot (2)
4. Repeat from other side for (3) and (4)

Note: Make passes "poke-able" as well as to get to slot lot player F2 for shot.

Key Points

- Lead with hands and stick
- Use of butterfly block to shot lane; then attack puck
- Behind-net tracking
- Goalie is not to lean away from post
- Keep hips, legs, and shoulders facing slot

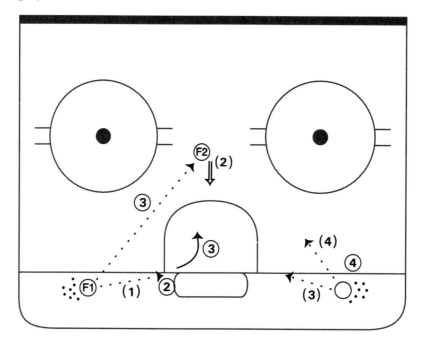

Short and Long Poke Check

12 pucks drill (3 pucks near posts each side, 6 in slot)
Goalie comes out with stick hand extended (hold stick at butt)

Sequence

1. Player tries to deke (1), and goalie tries to long poke check and play deke
2. Recover for short poke (2) (clear puck to corner)
3. Back out to play deke (3); continue as order of pucks shown: dekes: (1), (3), (5), (7), (9), (11): short poke checks: (2), (4), (6), (8), (10), (12)

Key Points

- Short poke check, use good post location
- Long poke check, keep stick extended
- Quick feet to pursue puck

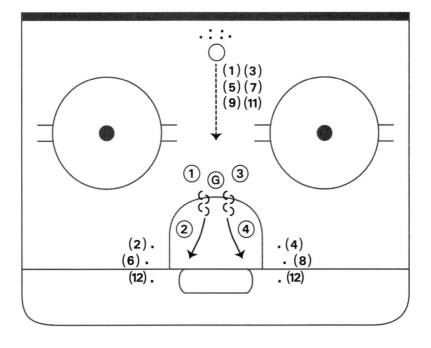

Lunge Poke Check

2-time repetition each way

Sequence

1. Goalie takes shot from F1 (1) and then F2 (2)
2. Player F1 sends soft/slow puck (3)
3. Challenge: between goalie and far-side player F4 for lunge poke check (4)
4. Recover to shot from F3 (5) and then shot from F4 (6)
5. Continue; restart from other side for sequence starting with F3

Key Points

- Gap control
- Skating lunge check
- Recoveries
- Timing challenges

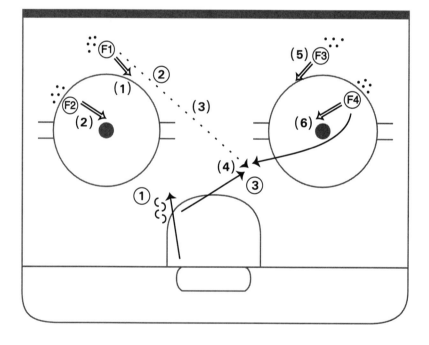

Puck Handling: Fielding

2 minutes

Sequence

1. Puck dumped in by F1
2. Goalie fields and passes puck to player F1, who stays and waits
3. Goalie recovers to play shot (2) by F2
4. Goalie recovers to play deke (4) by F1
5. Goalie recovers to repeat and continue same from this side
6. Continue alternating sides

Key Points

- Quick feet
- Pass to match level of play
- Back-to-net quickness and recovery
- Passes by goalie are "tape to tape"

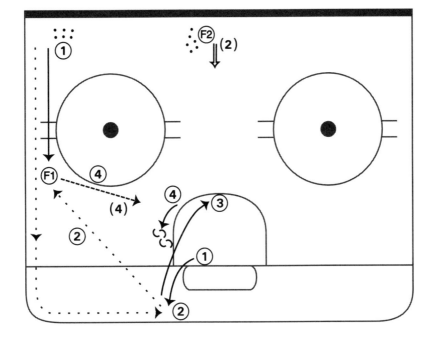

Puck Handling: Passing

2 minutes
Loose pucks behind net and stick length or
more from post (start at post)

Sequence

1. Goalie gets puck and passes (1), then quick return to net for shot (2) by F1
2. Out to challenge deke from slot (3); recover and pass (4) to F3
3. Quick return for shot (5) by F3; then out to challenge F2 for deke (6)
4. Continue alternating from post to post

Key Points

- Passing skills
- Gap control
- Use one- and two-handed passing techniques
- Quick recoveries to net and shot lane

208

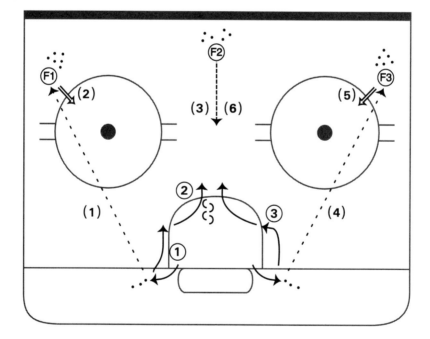

Appendix

Websites

Hockey Schools and Camps

Jim Corsi—jimcorsi.com
World Hockey Institute—worldhockeyinstitute.com
Roger Neilsen—rogerneilsonshockey.com
Minnesota Hockey Camp—mnhockeycamps.com
Hockey Ministries International—gospelcom.net/hmi/
Huron Hockey—huronhockey.com
Saves—savesgoaltending.com
Craig Billington—billingtongoalieschool.com
Jon Elkin—elkingoaltending.com
Rick Heinz—rickheinz.com
Mitch Korn—mitchkorn.com
Jim Park—jimpark.com
Vladislav Tretyak—goaltending.net

Equipment Manufacturers

Louisville—louisville-hockey.com
Bauer—bauer.com
Battram—battram.com
Brians—briansmfg.com
Brown—brownhockey.com
Itech—itech.com
Koho—koho.com
McKenney—mckenneysports.com
Simmons—donsimmons.com
Thomson—paulthomsonusa.com
Vaughn—vaughnhockey.com

Equipment Sales
Buffalo, NY—greatskate.com
Detroit, MI—peranis.com
Fort Erie, ON—reidsports.com
Garden Grove, CA—hockeygiant.com
London, Ontario—sourcelondon.com
New York, NY—goalstopperz.com
Rollinsford, NH—1800faceoff.com
Thorold, ON—frontrowsport.com
Vancouver, BC—cyclonetaylor.com
Vancouver, BC—thehockeyshop.com
Vancouver, BC—the-sports-exchange.com

Women-Specific Equipment Sales
Chick—chickwear.com
Rinky—rinky.com

Mask Design
Design Air—designair.net
Gunnarsson—daveart.com
Redick—redickmask.com
Voodoo—voodooair.com
Warwick—warwickgoaliemasks.com

General Information
Goalie Site—goalers.com
Goalie Site—icegoalie.com
Goalie Site—fromthecrease.com
Goalie Links—goaltending.net
Hockey Links—hockeyhost.com
Hockey Hall of Fame—hhof.com

Periodicals
Goalies World Magazine—goaliesworld.com
The Hockey News—thehockeynews.com
Junior Hockey—usajuniorhockey.com

Books and Videos
Amazon—amazon.com
Chapters—chapters.com
Sports Asylum—hockeybooks.com

Instruction and Coaching Aids
CanCoach—cancoach.com
Coaching Links—hockeycoach.com
Gold in the Net—goldinthenet.com
Mitron Systems—mitronhockey.com
PASS—passhockey.com

Training Aids
Puck Shooting Machine—boni.com
Miscellaneous Gadgets—mrassist.com

Accessories
Cool Hockey—coolhockey.com
Hocks—gohocks.com
River City Sports—rivercitysports.com
Jersey Express—jerseyexpress.com

Associations
USA Hockey—usahockey.com
Hockey Canada—canadianhockey.com
North American Teams—eteamz.com/icehockey/
Minor/Youth Hockey—your own local hockey association

Training Aids
Tennis balls—used in place of pucks on or off the ice to improve reaction and reflexes
Medicine balls—used off-ice to improve strength and flexibility
Deflection board—dense metal bar that is affixed to ice or wooden bench on its side. Used to simulate tips and deflections
Push-up blocks—used to increase upper-body strength

Free weights—used off-ice to improve strength and flexibility

Chin-up bar—used to improve shoulder, arms, back, and stomach muscles

Shooting machine (puck)—electricity-powered machine used on- or off-ice to simulate shots and passes (bonni.com)

Shooting machine (tennis ball)—electricity- or battery-powered machine used off-ice to simulate shots and improve reactions

Knee pads—use the volleyball or basketball knee pads for protection when doing off-ice tumbling exercises

Slide board—slick surface used to replicate skating motion (can help improve lateral movement)

Table tennis—can be a very effective way to improve tracking, reflexes, and hand-eye coordination (also helps foster competitive spirit)

Frequently Asked Questions

Q. *At what age should a young goalie transition to goalie skates?*

A. The child should learn how to skate with regular skates, which will teach him the all-important edge, or skate-blade, control. Seven- and eight-year-olds playing at Double Letter or Travel team levels should consider goalie skates, especially because these skates provide extra safety. In any case, a child learning to be a goaltender should be in goalie skates by nine years of age.

Q. *At what age should a child commit to playing goalie full time?*

A. Although a child may already have a strong desire to be a goaltender, learning the position is demanding and requires a strong commitment on the part of the child. Generally speaking, to develop the necessary skills, a child should be playing the position full time by the age of eight.. Do not lose sight of the importance of learning to skate. Some young players gravitate to goaltending because they are poor skaters. But even goalies need good skating skills and must work at acquiring them!

Q. *Should I buy new or used equipment?*

A. This is a personal choice and depends on the means of the parents, the association, and/or the sponsors. The most important thing is that you get complete equipment that fits properly and provides maximum protection.

Q. Should I try to put my child on a good or a bad team?

A. This choice generally isn't given to parents, but check out who the coach and the assistants are. Are learning and teaching priorities? Is "winning by any means" their motto? And remember: good goalies will make any team better.

Q. Should I ask the coach about letting my child play as a skater if the other goalie is scheduled to play?

A. Some associations have draft rules that prohibit this practice. However, at some levels, it is allowed. Playing "out" helps give a goalie a forward's perspective and will improve his skating skills.

Q. If I have questions or problems, what is the best way to approach the coach?

A. Begin with dialogue and communication with the coach from the start of the season. This way, when you talk to the coach, it's not *only* when there are problems. Always treat your child's coach with honesty and respect.

Q. Should I try to put my child on a team where he will be the only goalie?

213

A. Once again, you probably will not be able to choose. More importantly, you should try to make sure that a team's coaching philosophy and level of play suit the talent level of your child. Of course, if you are able to place your child on a team where he is the only goalie, it will mean constant ice time for him.

Q. Should I encourage my son to play other sports? To play goalie in these sports?

A. Yes. Encourage him to play other sports, but not necessarily only goal-oriented sports that have net minders. It's good to learn how to deal with the challenges presented by other sports and other positions.

Q. What should I do if my child's team doesn't have a goalie coach?

A. Approach the coach and suggest that some time be dedicated to goalie skills, either specifically or within team drills. Using this book, inform yourself about drills and methods for goalies, and share this information with your child's coach or encourage him to consult this book or his own resources.

Q. Should goalie skates be sharpened? If so, how often?

A. Goalies use fast starts and fast stops to track the play-action. Goalie skates must be sharp enough to allow the goalie good edge control and the ability to shuffle. Sharpen skates at least once every two to three weeks—although this varies depending on ice time, ice hardness, and the goalie's strength, size, and weight.

Additional Instructional Resources

Allaire, Francois. *Hockey Goaltending for Young Players*
Bellefleur, Bob. *Characteristics of Goaltending*
Bertnaga, Joseph. *Goaltending*
Brodeur, Dennis. *Guardians of the Net*
Chambers, Dave. *Complete Hockey Instruction*
Chambers, Dave. *Off-Ice Summer Training Program*
Daccord, Brian. *Hockey Goaltending*
Dryden, Dave. *Coaching Goaltenders*
Dryden, Dave. *Technical Aspects of Goaltending*
Fischler, Stan. *Hot Goalies*
Fuhr, Grant. *Fuhr on Goaltending*
Lemire, Vic. *Goaltenders Are Not Targets*
Percival, Lloyd. *The Hockey Handbook*
Plante, Jacques. *On Goaltending*
Rossiter, Sean. *Goaltending: Hockey the NHL Way*
Smith, Don. *Goalie: Man Behind the Mask*
Tretyak, V. *The Art of Goaltending*
Young, Ian. *Behind the Mask*

Books For Goalies

Aaseng, Nathan. *Hockey's Fearless Goalies*
Brophy, Mike. *Curtis Joseph: The Acrobat*
Blysma, Dan and Blysma, Jay. *So Your Son Wants to Play in the NHL*
Blysma, Dan and Blysma, Jay. *So You Want to Play in the NHL*
Burgan, Mike. *Dominik Hasek*
Call, Ken and Kramer, Sydelle. *In the Cage: Four Goalie Greats*
Duplacey, James. *Great Goalies: NHL*

Duplacey, James. *Hockey's Hottest Goalies*

Dupuis, David. *Sawchuck: The Triumphs and Troubles of the World's Greatest Goalie*

Field, Ross and Garrison, Ross. *Game Face: Goalie Mask Coloring Book (NHL Hockey)*

Fischler, Stan. *Goalies: Legends from the NHL's Toughest Job*

Hughes, Morgan. *Patrick Roy: Champion Goalie*

Hunter, Douglas. *A Breed Apart: An Illustrated History of Goaltending*

Irvin, Dick. *In the Crease: Goaltenders Look at Life in the NHL*

Mason, Gary and Gunn, Barbara. *Guardians: The Secret Life of Goalies*

Orr, Frank. *Great Goalies of Pro Hockey*

Rossiter, Sean. *Dominik Hasek*

Schnakenberg, Robert. *Martin Brodeur*

Stewart, Mark. *Martin Brodeur*

Thomas, Linda. *Meet the Goalies: Hockey*

Thorne, Ian. *Great Goalies (Stars of the National Hockey League)*

Tretyak, Vladislav. *The Hockey I Love*

Index